French

D0400683

Also by Rob Hunter:

Winter Skills (Constable)
The Outdoor Companion (Constable)
Walking in France (Oxford Illustrated Press)
Map and Compass (Spur)
Lightweight Camping (Spur)

and as Neil Lands:

A Visitor's Guide to the Dordogne (Moorland)
A Visitor's Guide to Brittany (Moorland)
Languedoc-Roussillon (Spur)
Burgundy (Spur)
Beyond the Dordogne (Spur)
The French Pyrénées (Spur)
Normandy (Nicholson)

# ROB HUNTER

MULLER, BLOND & WHITE

First published in Great Britain in 1984 by Frederick Muller.
Reprinted in 1986 by Muller, Blond & White
55 Great Ormond Street
London WC1N 3HZ.

Copyright © Rob Hunter 1984

All rights reserved. No part of this publication may be
reproduced, stored in a retrieval system, or transmitted in
any form or by any means, electronic, mechanical,
photocopying, recording or otherwise, without the prior
consent of Muller, Blond & White Limited.

British Library Cataloguing in Publication Data

Hunter, Rob
    Cycle touring in France.
    1. Cycling—France—Handbooks, manuals, etc.
    2. France—Handbooks, manuals, etc.
    I. Title
    914.4'04838'0247966        DC17

    ISBN 0-584-11080-4

Line drawings and maps by Terry Brown.
Photographs by Rob Hunter and the French Government
Tourist Office, London.

Printed in Great Britain by
Redwood Burn Ltd., Trowbridge, Wiltshire

# CONTENTS

# LIST OF ILLUSTRATIONS

# ACKNOWLEDGMENTS

A great many people have helped me with this book, but I would particularly like to thank the following for their advice and encouragement: Tom Vernon; Richard Ballantine of *Bicycle Magazine*; John Wilcockson of *Cyclist Monthly*; Austin Grey, Touring Officer of the C.T.C.; Eve Livet of Lyon, France; John Lloyd of *Practical Camper*; John Potter of Bike Events; Susi Madron; John Kettley of The London Bicycle Company; Holdsworth Cycles and Raleigh T.I.; Karrimor Ltd; Jane Larcombe of P & O Ferries; Toby Oliver of Brittany Ferries; and among cycletourists in France, George Ansell, Mark Ringwood, Steve Bergson, Marc Mentonville, Gordon Halker, Mike Goffin, Peter Toothill of Switzerland, G. Thornington of Jersey; Phillip Pond of *Camping*; and as always, Estelle Huxley, who can read my handwriting.

The publishers would like to thank the French Government Tourist Office for permission to reproduce the photographs on pages: 68, 77, 83, 93, 100, 102, 103, 107, 109, 112, 119, 125, 129, 130, 145, 150, 172.

# FOREWORD
# by Tom Vernon

Cycling through France is one of the great romantic experiences of life, weather permitting. It is an affair of serenity rather than tempest.

There are other countries bigger, more dramatic, more exotic, but France – like the bicycle – is perfectly adapted to humanity. The French – by no means alone among nations – have a natural tendency to assume that the world has been organised for their particular benefit, and where France herself has failed to meet this criterion, France has had to change. The result is a harmony of pastoral countryside, formally-inclined forests, wildernesses which are neither tame nor too far from civilisation, old towns, rivers whose banks are made for anglers, and roads fit for the solitary and self-propelled.

There are so many little, quiet roads, and even in the mountains the gradients have none of the viciousness of many British hills. They are long, but leisurely, for – again like the bicycle – they have been made for human legs. Picnic food is the best in the world; food shops and markets a delight for those who prefer to set the quality of their eating by enjoyment, rather than by the convenience of a manufacturer. Good restaurants, reasonable hotels, nice places to camp, wine . . . and, often, sun abound.

Most great romantic experiences can survive a certain amount of bad weather, but few love affairs remain unharmed by bad organisation. Bomb off on any old bone-shaker down a *Route Nationale*, and it will not be delightful at all, nor will it be an enduring relationship if you happen to split a tube and have not learnt in advance that French bike shops don't sell your kind of tyres. You don't want to waste a precious holiday discovering what could have made it a good one. Do you know what gears you want? Unless you do, your bike almost certainly has not got them. Do you know what to take? And where do you think you're going?

Rob Hunter knows France and cycling, and is pretentious about neither. (One of the other things guaranteed to ruin a love affair is swank.) I have cycled from one end of France to the other, but he has found things to tell me I never knew before, both about the country and my bike. I wish I had had such a book before I set off – and, when I cycle there again, I will read it before I go, especially for the routes and the advice on what to carry. But – most important of all – because Rob, too, is in love with this loveable land he consequently has the best possible qualification as a guide to her favours.

'I have discovered that most of the beauties of travel are due to the strange hours we keep to see them.'
*William Carlos Williams*

# Introduction

**'Every man has two countries; his own
and France.'**

This is a book about France. More precisely it is a book about
cycletouring in France: seeing that exciting and enjoyable
country at a natural pace, while rolling gently from one place
to another, having fun, meeting people, seeing the sights. For
all these reasons, cycletouring in France is now my favourite
occupation, but I came to it late and it might help to set the
scene and the style of this book if I were to begin by explaining
how it began and why I enjoy it.

For many years I have wandered France on foot or toured
there by car, but as time went by I discovered that both methods
of travel had certain inbuilt snags. Walking is too slow, and
while I bow to no one in my love of the hills, I came to wonder
if staggering over the mountains under a heavy pack was as
great as I had made it out to be. On the other hand, car travel,
while fast and comfortable, is increasingly expensive and more
seriously, cuts the traveller off from people. I like travelling,
and in the end travelling is about people, meeting people,
different people, and becoming, if only for a short while, a part
of their lives. Arrive in a small French village afoot or on a
cycle and you instantly become part of the social scene. The
French love eccentrics just as much in reality as the English
are said to do in theory, and any cyclist, any foreigner, and
above all, any British cyclist is, by his very presence, an object
of interest. From that ice-breaking beginning, much may flow.
The French, whatever you may have heard to the contrary, are
an hospitable and friendly people, providing you accept them
on their terms and make a little effort, which usually means
speaking at least a little French and letting that British reserve
melt a little.

It also happens that the French are a great cycling nation.
After all, what cyclist has not heard of the Tour de France?
There are some ten million active cyclists in France, three
times as many as there are in Britain, although our national
populations are just about the same, and the cycling facilities

are therefore excellent. No town is without its bike shop and the roads, especially the minor roads, are full of cyclists at weekends, while those elements which so plague cyclists in Britain, the motorists, are notably less aggressive in France, probably because the drivers are also cyclists themselves.

Cycletouring in France is therefore a relaxed and enjoyable pastime, the ideal way to spend a holiday, and all you really need, apart from this book, is a bike.

This book is divided into three parts. The first chapter deals with the basic elements of cycletouring—the cycle, the clothing, the equipment, the preparation—and would apply wherever you choose to go touring. I have to say at once that the opinions expressed on machines, equipment and techniques are my own, although I have had them checked by experts and adjusted them where necessary. I have advertised for advice in the cycling press, picked the brains of any experienced cyclist I happened to meet, and from the subsequent welter of assistance – for cyclists are a helpful lot – chosen what I believe represents an accurate and, I hope, helpful selection of information. It can *only* be a selection, and those who seek more advice on any particular aspect of cycling must look to one of the books listed in the bibliography.

The second section covers cycletouring facilities in France: transportation, accommodation, how to plan a tour there, and the accumulated advice of scores of Francophile cyclists plus that of the author who has, for the last twenty years, spent every spare moment in France, the country of his heart.

The third section of this book consists of 20 cycle tours in France, including at the finish a ride from the Channel to the Mediterranean. These trips are designed not just to offer good cycling and suitable tours for any competent cyclist, but also to display a wide cross-section of my beloved France, on tours to all parts, either circular, lateral or thematic.

Three final points: Firstly, I am *not* a *passionate* cyclist. I do not worship the Gods of the Cotterless Chainset. I cycle because I enjoy it, and that to me seems reason enough. The title describes the objects of this book and those seeking a work crammed with information on the more arcane aspects of sprocket-fangling are reading the wrong book. Secondly, as a pre-emptive strike against the critics, I have spent the best part of two years researching this book, trying bikes, attending maintenance classes, visiting factories, and best of all, touring in France. The facts and opinions expressed have been studied and broadly approved by those who know more about the mechanics of cycling than I (or most readers) will ever need to know, and as far as they go they are thought correct. All cyclists will know, and all new cyclists will quickly learn, how wide are the opinions held on almost every aspect of this enjoyable sport and how passionately every stated point will be debated. Rude letters are anticipated, but does a point of detail really matter? Surely Robert Louis Stevenson spoke for all travellers when he said, 'I travel for travel's sake. The great affair is to move'.

Finally, I am a travel writer and, as you may have guessed, a Francophile. I have enjoyed researching and writing this book, and to the names mentioned in the acknowledgements may I also add a word of thanks to those many unknown and unknowing cyclists, French and English, whom I met on my travels and who waited patiently to have their brains well picked. We were having a good time, cycletouring in France, and if you get as much fun out of it as we have had, then this book will have been worth while, so . . .

*Bon voyage en vélo*

*Rob Hunter*
*1984*

# Chapter 1
# Start Cycletouring

'La distance n'y fait rien: il n'y a que le premier pas qui coute.' *Mme Deffand*

---

All you really need to start cycletouring is a bike. Within quite broad limits almost any machine will do, at least for shorter tours, and those interested in taking up this fascinating hobby and who already have a cycle, might as well start out on the one they have before investing in a specialised touring machine; a few day tours of up to 80km (50 miles) or so will soon reveal the limitations of the present bike and give the tourist some ideas on the sort of touring machine required. If you are lucky, maybe the one you already have actually *is* a touring machine.

The would-be cycletourist usually has three main choices at the start: to use an existing machine which may or may not be suitable; to have one specially built for touring by one of Britain's many specialist cycle-builders; or to buy a good, proven, touring machine off-the-peg, and adapt it slightly to suit his or her particular size, tastes and requirements. For the purposes of this book, and from my own experience, I have chosen to illustrate the last alternative here. My original machine was not right so I changed it. I lacked the knowledge to specify my requirements for a hand-built machine and, it must be admitted, I also lacked the cash, so I chose to buy a touring machine made by a well-established manufacturer and purchased from my local specialist bike shop. I have not regretted this course of action and I commend it to you.

Cycles fall into three broad categories, and are generally designed either for commuting, racing or touring. Those attracted by the idea of cycletouring will definitely find the experience much more enjoyable on a machine designed for the job, so in this chapter we will examine the touring machine, the ancillary clothing and equipment needed for touring, and those U.K.-based organisations which will assist the cyclist to start touring, first at home and later abroad.

First though, the cycle which—if designed and adjusted for our purpose—will give many miles of safe, comfortable riding across the fair land of France. The main components are detailed below but begin by studying Fig. 1 and learning the names of parts.

It might be as well to mention here that the Imperial measure is still generally used in the cycling world, although metric is creeping in here and there. I will use both as circumstances or common practice dictate.

**Fig. 1**  The main components of a bicycle

**FRAME**  The touring frame should be made from high-quality steel tubing, either high-carbon tempered, or even better, a steel alloy such as carbon-manganese, chrome-manganese, or the manganese-molybdenum used for that popular tubing, Reynolds 531, seen on most quality British bikes. These metallurgical terms can be confusing. Certainly on the main tubes and forks the tubing should be 'double butted', that is, thicker at the ends than in the middle. Most stress falls at the ends of the tubes (see Fig. 2) and 'double butted' tubing offers extra strength at the ends, lighter weight at the mid sections, and a more flexible, responsive frame. Incidentally, the butting is internal.

ORDINARY TUBING          DOUBLE BUTTED TUBING

**Fig. 2**

Whether tubes should be lugged, that is, fitted into sockets at the ends, is more debatable, but my advice is that at least the main tubes, seat, down, head and top tube (crossbar) should be lugged. A touring frame is usually longer than that used on racing machines, and to the accustomed eye the difference from a racing machine is instantly apparent. A touring cycle has mudguards. A touring machine also looks longer. A cyclist, mounting a touring machine for the first time, will be surprised at the distance between saddle and front wheel. This is because good touring machines have a long wheelbase of around 41–41.5in from the front fork-ends to the rear fork-ends and the forks are raked forward. This long wheelbase is a major factor in a comfortable ride and makes the bike easy to handle when carrying a heavy load.

Another critical element is the seat tube and head tube angle. Both angles are measured between the front of the head tube and the front of the rear tube, and an imaginary line parallel to the ground. This is already becoming complicated, as mechanical matters so easily can, so let it suffice to state that a good touring frame will have a 41in wheelbase and a 71° or 72° head-seat tube angle. If those elements are present in the specification and the frame is soundly constructed and well finished in some high grade steel alloy like Reynolds 531, then the touring cyclist has all the essential elements for a good frame.

LUGGED FRAME

**Fig. 3**

**CHAIN-STAYS** Chain-stay length is yet another frame element which affects the suitability for touring. Longer chain-stays mean a more flexible frame and improve the position of loaded panniers, shifting them a little further forward of the rear axle. Touring chain-stays should be between 17.5 and 18in long.

**FORK RAKE** Fork rake is another essential element and the front forks on a touring machine will be raked forward more than those on a racing machine. Fork rake is defined as the amount of forward bend, the difference between a straight vertical line from the headset and the front wheel axle. Something in excess of 2in of fork rake is desirable and makes for a smoother ride.

**FRAME SIZE** Frame size is very important. The accepted criteria for selecting a frame size is the cyclist's inside leg measurement less 9in. My inside leg measures 32in and my cycle therefore has a 23.5in frame, the saddle being adjusted to absorb the odd .5in. Some shops apply an even simpler test and suggest that the frame is right when the cyclist can straddle the top tube with nearly an inch to spare. Minor adjustments can be made by changing the handlebar stem, or altering the position and height of the saddle. We will come to these adjustments later, but the basic frame should fit.

Those machines selected by women or children may be smaller in every way than those chosen by an average-sized male, but the elements and guidelines listed here remain true, even on a 'mixte' machine, a model designed for women, with slanting rather than horizontal top-tubes. Many ladies now ride diamond frame 'male' machines, which are, of course, stronger. Before accepting any bike, even a well-known make, carry out a careful examination of the frame, noting the brazing at the joints, the paint finish, the general standard of frame construction. This will give useful clues to the craftsmanship employed in the construction, and if the finish is shoddy, reject the bike.

**WHEELS** Next to the frame the wheels are the most critical part of the machine, and the part most prone to problems. Wheels can be broken down into various component parts: hubs, spokes, rims and tyres, with the tyres consisting of the outer cover and the inner tube. Each component should be selected to enhance the touring potential of the machine. Money spent on top-quality wheels is the best investment you can make.

**Hubs** These come either small or large flange; the flange being the point where the spokes are attached to the hub. Large flange hubs mean a shorter spoke and probably a stronger wheel, while small flange hubs offer a *marginally* weaker wheel but a more comfortable ride. Most cycletourists don't worry too much about flange size. One useful wheel feature when you will have to get a bike on and off planes and trains, is *quick-release hubs*. They are also useful when you have to mend a flat tyre or want to stow the cycle in the car boot.

**Spokes** Spokes are usually made from galvanised steel, and there are normally 36 spokes to the wheel, although 40 spokes are not uncommon. Spokes can come plain gauge or double-butted, the last being somewhat stronger. The spokes should be 14-gauge or, for double-butted spokes (which I recommend for cycle-camping especially) 14/16 gauge. The wheel strength also depends on the meshing of the spokes, or how many times one spoke will cross another between rim and hub. Three-cross meshing is most common.

**Rims** The less weight in the wheel the better, and aluminium alloy rims are the best choice. Modern alloys are just as strong as steel, and married to the right brake blocks, alloy rims will also offer better stopping power in wet weather. Touring rims will be wider than those on racing wheels. Super Champion or Weinmann rims are just two good makes.

Before moving on to tyres, it is worth stressing here that the strength of a wheel depends as much on the construction as on the component materials. Wheel building is an art, and a poorly built wheel will provide the tourist with a succession of bent rims and broken spokes. If the spokes keep breaking it's time to go back to the bike shop for double-butted spoking and to have the wheel rebuilt.

**Tyres** The best tyres (covers) for the touring cyclist are those with wire-on rims and an inner tube. The popular size is 27in × 1.25in, or the metric 700c. These look alike, but the 700c is in fact 4mm smaller, and they are not interchangeable. It's also worth mentioning that the individual tyre manufacturers' sizes also vary and one company's 27in × 1.25in can differ from that of another. Continental tyre and tube sizes differ from those commonly used on U.K.–built machines and so I *always* carry a spare cover and two spare inner tubes as part of my basic touring kit when cycletouring in France.

**HANDLEBARS** Most touring cyclists choose drop handlebars, even if they rarely go down 'on the drops', the lowest riding position. Most tourers steer instead from the top of the bars, or from the top of the brake levers. It is, however, useful to have the variety of positions offered by drop handlebars, and going 'on the drops' is always a good idea when plugging hard into a head-wind or going downhill. Straight handlebars are a perfectly valid alternative and the experienced tourer will often choose the slightly raised *randonneur* drop-bars which offer a very comfortable upright riding position as well as the drops. I also recommend that *after* finding a suitable position for the brakes the tourer fits the handlebars with thick padding such as 'Grab On', which reduces road shock and can prove a real boon to pounded palms on a long tour (see Fig. 4).

GRAB ON HANDLEBAR PADDING

**Fig. 4**

**BRAKES** Good brakes are clearly essential for the loaded cycletourist. Touring bikes will have cable brakes, and while most experts recommend centre-pull cable brakes, side-pull are equally effective. I personally find dual-safety levers useful while admitting that they do not have the power of the main-brake lever. A useful feature which comes in handy when adjusting the brakes or removing the wheel is a brake lever with brake-block release, a small lever which lets the brakes open out clear of the rim. Fit the brake levers with rubber brake hoods, and so gain another comfortable riding position.

Brake cables stretch, especially when new, and if the brakes are to work efficiently the tourist must tighten up the cables every few days when on a tour.

**BRAKE BLOCKS** Brake blocks are the sharp end of the braking process and will repay attention. Aztec blocks are useful for both alloy and steel rims and work well in wet or dry conditions. Scott Malthauser blocks also work in the wet, but must only be used with alloy rims. Check rims and blocks carefully, for using the wrong brake block can ruin a rim. Brake blocks must be changed once they are worn down. If they squal, check that there is no oil on the rims or have the block 'toe'd in' slightly at the front, bending the clamp *gently* with a pair of pliers.

**SADDLE** At one time I had no less than five saddles, each purchased in the search for a comfortable ride. Dark thoughts of transplant surgery loomed ever larger, as my rear-end and the saddles failed to come to terms. Wide, sprung-mattress saddles may look comfortable but they just won't do; you need a narrow, leather or leather-covered model, and you need to get used to it. There are various types of saddle on the market, some, such as the Madison, with 'anatomic' padding designed to support the bones of the pelvis, but after a few thousand miles and much discomfort, I have come to favour a well broken-in Brooks B17 Standard leather saddle as the best saddle for the committed tourist. It is important to select the saddle with care, for the leather of my first saddle was so thick that even 500 miles of riding failed to soften it at all, and my eyes continued to water.

My present saddle was first softened by rubbing in a whole tin of Proofhide and applying a little neat foot-oil to the underside. I then rode on it at every opportunity and eventually it became very comfortable. There is no real short cut to comfort, but a well broken-in, leather saddle will give a comfortable ride and last for years. It is also worth pointing out that the only way to avoid saddle-soreness is to ride enough to get the rear-end used to the saddle, as well as the other way round.

**CRANKS AND PEDALS** Cranks and pedals get a lot of wear and tear, besides being exposed to abrasion from road spray and grit. All ten-speed cranksets are alloy and usually cotterless, but that apart they vary widely. The cranks give leverage to the pedal action, and while size depends on the rider, but 165 or 170 mm cranks are about right. Pedals should be metal and must be fitted with toe-clips.

**GEARS** Choosing the correct mix of gears is an essential decision but often the most difficult one for the touring cyclist. Let's begin by stating that a touring machine needs ten gears. You can find bikes with three, five, 12, 15, even 18 gears, but ten is about right for our purpose. It is common practice to express the gear ratios in inches and the inches are therefore calculated as follows:

$$\frac{\text{teeth on chainwheel}}{\text{teeth on freewheel sprocket}} \times \text{wheel diameter} = \text{gear ratio}$$

Therefore:

$$\frac{52 \text{ teeth (chainwheel)}}{13 \text{ tooth (rear sprocket)}} \times 27\text{in wheel} = 108\text{in}$$

Precisely why this inch scale was originally arrived at need not concern us, for we are only concerned here with finding suitable gear ratios for touring. The Americans and the French tend to like 15 gears, using a third chainwheel, but most British cyclists stick to ten gears, which is perfectly adequate for the tours offered in this book, provided the range of gears is correct. When purchasing a machine the tourist should find out the ratios, expressed as here, in inches, and see if the range of gears is wide enough for the type of touring he or she has in mind . . . and here we hit a snag.

The choice of gears is a highly personal matter. It depends on many factors; the rider's fitness, the type of riding and speed preferred, whether the cyclist goes day-touring or on loaded, extended camping trips, and last but by no means least, on the wind, the weather and the terrain. Anyone contemplating a long summer tour over mountains such as the Hautes Alpes or Pyrénées, will need at least one very low gear for climbing, but even for touring in normal terrain the cyclist needs a wide range of ratios stepped down regularly from top to bottom, one of which will offer a suitable gear for the terrain being crossed at any particular moment.

Hours can be spent working out suitable ratios, but I have come to feel, *for me*, that a high of around 85, and a low somewhere in the upper twenties, is about right for *loaded Continental touring*. A high gear is always useful for those flat roads or for when the wind is behind, or for riding over switchback roads where pedalling hard in a high gear down one hill goes a long way towards carrying you up the next one, and a low 'granny' gear means that if you keep at it, the top of the col will eventually appear. Also, after a few days on tour even the most unprepared rider will find the legs getting stronger and start to wish for a different range of gears. Most off-the-peg cycles are too highly geared for loaded touring. My original gears were:

|    | 14    | 18   | 23   | 32   | 34   |
|----|-------|------|------|------|------|
| 52 | 100.2 | 78   | 61   | 43   | 41   |
| 42 | 81    | 62.9 | 49.1 | 35.4 | 33.2 |

For cycle touring in France I changed the front rings from 52/42 to 42/36, and got the following ratios, without changing the expensive rear block:

|    | 14   | 18   | 23   | 32   | 34   |
|----|------|------|------|------|------|
| 42 | 81   | 62.9 | 49   | 35.4 | 33   |
| 36 | 67.5 | 54   | 40.5 | 29   | 27   |

A trifle on the low side perhaps, but ideal for long hill climbs in hot weather.

Gear levers are traditionally placed on the down tube, which suits me, but they can be fitted to the stem, or at the end of the handlebars.

The best advice is to buy a bike and ride it until you feel able to decide on any necessary changes to the gear ratios. This will usually be at one end or the other and a change of one cog may make all the difference. Since any *dérailleur* can only cope with a limited number of changes, consult the bike shop about your requirements and listen to their advice before you make any drastic alterations. Good makes of *dérailleur* include Shimano, Suntour, Huret, Simplex and Campagnola.

**BITS AND PIECES** If the elements mentioned above have been carefully chosen, or are present on the machine you purchase, then the touring cycle has all the basics necessary for enjoyable touring. There remain, however, a number of other useful items. 'Grab On' handlebar padding has been mentioned. The wise tourist will fit a rear-view mirror, and the Mirrycle is ideal (see Fig. 5). This need not be swapped to the left side of the handlebars for Continental touring. A pump is essential and best fitted to the front of the seat tube. If it is fitted under the crossbar or behind the seat tube, the tourist will be continually pulling it off when lifting the machine. Cycles are expensive items, so carry a lock and chain and never leave the cycle unlocked. The Citadel lock is excellent, but heavy, so I prefer a long plastic-covered chain secured with a combination lock. This combination type of lock avoids the risk you run of losing the key to a padlock just after the bike has been securely attached to a lamp-post in, say, Strasbourg. Spare lamp bulbs and a plastic bag, to protect the saddle from the rain or in transit, are also useful.

All touring bikes in France must be fitted with a reflector,

THE MIRRYCLE

Fig. 5

lights and a bell or horn. Many tourists like dynamo-powered lights, but I prefer dry-cell battery lamps, partly because I dislike dynamo-drag on the wheels, but mostly because I rarely cycle after dark but often need a light to find my way about the campsite. With a dynamo, when the wheels stop turning the lights go out, but a battery lamp makes a useful torch.

**SUMMARY** The good touring cycle should have:

**Frame** A strong, flexible steel frame, with as much double-butting as possible throughout, particularly in the main tubes, and these should be lugged. Look out for the following specifics:
Head/seat tube angle: 72°/71°
Fork rake: 2in minimum
Wheelbase: 41in minimum
Chain-stay length: 17.5in minimum.

**Wheels** Alloy rims, 36-spoke, preferably double-butted, quick release. Mudguards are essential.

**Tyres** Wire-on, 27in × 1.25in. Carry two spare tubes and a spare cover.

**Fig. 6** The specifics

**Handlebars** Preferably randonneur but always 'drops', fitted with 'Grab On' padding. Fit a Mirrycle.

**Saddle** Leather. Brooks B17 Standard or Madison anatomic.

**Brakes** Centre-pull, with or without dual-safety levers, fitted with rubber brake hoods and, if possible, brake block release.

**Crankset** Alloy, cotterless. Pedals fitted with toe-clips.

**Gears** Ten-speed, top around 85in, bottom around 27in. Suntour 'Cyclone' and Campagnola 'Rally' are good makes.

**MAKES AND PRICES** Luckily, the cycletourist is well served by the main cycle manufacturers, most of whom produce a specially designed touring machine, and those looking for a suitable cycle have a wide choice even from the following selection:

| | |
|---|---|
| *Claude Butler* | Dalesman or Ladydale |
| *Coventry Eagle* | 531 Success |
| *Dawes* | Super Galaxy or Lady Super Galaxy |
| *Falcon* | Olympic or Super |
| *Holdsworth* | Mistral or Lady Mistral |
| *Peugeot* | Explorer or Lady Topaz |
| *Raleigh* | Royal or Royale |

Those seeking a tandem can consider the Gitane Randonnée.

**Prices** In this inflationary age, prices are difficult to specify, but competition means that cycle prices are keen and relatively stable. Anyone purchasing a good touring machine, off the peg, should expect to pay, at current prices, something between £200 and £300. Anything much less may be suspect, anything more a little extravagant, but there are discounts available. A study of the advertisements in the cycling magazines (see Bibliography) may prove rewarding.

**WHERE TO BUY YOUR CYCLE** The best place to purchase a touring cycle is from your nearest specialist cycle shop. If the shop belongs to the National Association of Cycle Traders (N.A.C.T.) so much the better. Shops which sell cycles as just one item among others will not be able to offer the necessary advice before purchase, or the necessary servicing afterwards. Cultivating a local N.A.C.T. shop provides the cyclist with a useful local contact for rapid servicing, repairs and advice. So, as a basic rule, support your local cycle shop.

The second piece of advice for use at the time of purchase is 'always buy the best you can afford'. Those who decide to cut corners and get a cheap machine will usually regret it later and decide to purchase a better machine, often losing money on the exchange.

Any machine will need a little 'customising', for, while the basic cycle is the same, all the customers are different. Handlebar stems may need to be altered, saddles raised or lowered, gears altered or exchanged. Certain parts may prove unsatisfactory after a few score miles and need replacement. The sensible tourist will arrange with his cycle shop at the time of purchase, to return with the machine after riding it for a hundred miles or so, so that it can be given a good service and any small but essential adjustments carried out. The cycle must be comfortable to ride and a little adjustment here and there can make all the difference.

**FITTING CYCLE TO RIDER** Over the years, cyclists have discovered two rough rules of thumb which ensure that rider and machine are well suited:
1. The correct fore and aft distance from saddle to handlebars is when, with the cyclist's elbow against the tip of the saddle, the outstretched fingertips touch the handlebars.
2. The saddle is at the right height and leg-power maximised when, with the pedal at its lowest point, the rider, sitting in the saddle, can rest his heel on the pedal with the knee *slightly* bent. There should be 1.5–2″ of seat-pillar showing.

Get these two points correct and the riding position should be efficient and comfortable (see also page 20).

**MAINTENANCE AND SERVICING** Good touring cycles are not cheap and should be looked after. In addition they get a lot of wear and tear, and road grit and spray will rapidly reduce the value and effectiveness of the machine unless it is regularly serviced.

The first rule is that the cycle should be kept clean and the working and moving parts *lightly* oiled and free from grit. Clean the cycle after every ride and it will never get too dirty.

Main bearings, hubs, cranks and pedals should be dismantled, cleaned and, if necessary, re-packed with grease at least every six months or before any major tour. At this time any worn parts can be checked and if necessary replaced.

Wire cables stretch and when new will need fairly constant adjustment if the brakes and gears are to be kept in efficient working order. Apart from being a sensible thing to do, such regular servicing will teach the touring cyclist how to maintain and repair the machine on the road without the need for a bike shop. Fortunately France is well supplied with cycle shops, but even so, some running repairs may be necessary.

The tourist *must* be able to execute the following tasks.
1. Cleaning and oiling the working parts of the machine.
2. Puncture repair; tyre and tube replacement.
3. Brake and gear cable adjustment and replacement.
4. Stripping, cleaning, re-packing and reassembling hubs, cranks and bracket.
5. Spoke replacement.
6. Elementary wheel true-ing.

Wheel true-ing, like wheel building, is something of an art, but if a spoke breaks on a loaded bike the wheel will usually go out of true. When this happens, the wheel wobble may prevent the wheel passing the chain-stays or the brake blocks. This is where the brake-block release comes in handy, although it means that the cyclist is reduced to only one brake. It is usually advisable to stop, replace the spoke and true-up the wheel as much as possible, using the chain-stay arms as a guide. The final adjustment can be made at the next cycle shop.

If the broken spoke is on the chain-wheel side, spoke repair may be difficult, since to get a new spoke in, the block has to be removed. A well-built wheel is the best solution.

Learning these basic skills is not too difficult, for cycles are simple mechanical devices, but correct servicing does call for fine adjustment if the maintenance is not to do more harm than good.

Hub nuts, for example, must be tightened so that the wheel spins freely but the hub itself is not loose and able to vibrate. Getting the balance right between these two limits calls for experience and a fine touch.

## BASIC TOOL KIT
1. Allen key, 5, 6, 7mm.
2. Spanners, ring-open ended, 8-9-10-11-12-13-14mm.
3. Spoke nipple key (spare spokes)
4. Chain rivet extractor
5. Brake and gear cables (for long rear brake and gear—can be cut down if necessary)
6. Tyre levers
7. Freewheel remover
8. Chainset spanner and extractor
9. Screwdriver
10. Campagnola T-Spanner
11. Adjustable spanner
12. Two spare inner tubes, one cover
13. Spare blocks and shoes
14. Puncture repair outfit
15. Spanners to fit lockring and bottom bracket cups.
16. Grease-solvent (swafega) in small can.

With this equipment quite sophisticated maintenance is possible, but the weight is considerable and none of the tools will be of any use if you don't know how to use them. I take far fewer tools on French cycletours (see tour 20).

**MAINTENANCE BOOKS AND CLASSES** My advice is that all would-be tourists should devote the winter months to attending cycle maintenance classes at an evening institute. These are often run by the local bike shop or cycle club, and here, under skilled, or at least experienced supervision, the tourist can learn to service, dismantle and reassemble the machine. This is what I did and I found a 12-week course—one evening a week—most useful. Weekend runs with my classmate, also added to the experience.

Those with a more mechanical bent may be able to learn what to do from books, and a list of titles offering detailed advice on bike maintenance is given in one of the appendices. Cycle clubs, or some of the members of such clubs, will also teach the tourist to maintain the machine, and if all this fails to appeal, the cycle can always go back to the cycle shop for regular maintenance. Even so, the skills listed above must be grasped by every tourist, for cycletouring is more than usually prone to Murphy's Law, the one which states that 'If anything can go wrong, it will, and at the most unfortunate moment'. So learn cycle maintenance; it will probably pay off on your very first tour.

\* \* \*

Before we proceed any further let us just review how far we have come towards cycletouring in France. By now the tourist will have bought a suitable machine, ridden it for a hundred miles or so, had it serviced and adjusted or adapted it to his or her particular requirements, and, I hope, learned how to clean and maintain the machine, and is able to carry out adjustments and minor repairs. If this stage has been reached then the time has come to put together the necessary touring equipment, buy some suitable clothing, and plan some initial tours.

**CYCLING CLOTHING** Traditionally, cycling clothing is brightly coloured to attract the attention of myopic motorists, close-fitting to cut down wind resistance, and partially windproof to keep the cold out. Outfits like this can be seen on any weekend, worn by cyclists on club runs, and such clothing is equally suitable for long-distance touring at home and abroad.

Personally, while I have specially designed cycling clothing, I frequently go out on quite long tours in nothing more formal than T-shirt, tennis shorts and a pair of 'trainers', and if the truth were told I don't think that clothing matters, at least until the weather turns chilly. There are three exceptions to this sweeping statement, in that I always wear gloves for fear of a fall, I have a set of rain gear, and I wouldn't discourage anyone from wearing a helmet. That said, let us now look at cycling clothing, both the formal and the informal kind.

**Shoes** Cycling shoes usually are light, flat-soled with soft uppers and are very comfortable. They can be fitted with 'plates', metal slides which grip the rat-trap pedals and hold the foot correctly in place, but these plates are something of a frill and make a terrible noise when the cyclist is tip-toeing round a Gothic cathedral. The cycletourist will be better equipped with those cycle shoes which have a small heel and a stiff steel shank across the instep, like the Brancale cycle shoe, or a pair of 'trainers' provided the trainer fits the toe clip neatly and can be swiftly removed from the pedal in an emergency. I tend to wear socks, or long stockings in the chillier spring months, but they are not really needed in summer. A set of rainproof overshoes, are also useful.

**Shorts and trousers** The essential feature of 'proper' cycling shorts or trousers is a wide chamois-leather or terry-towelling patch sewn into the seat, which pads out to cover the trouser seams and helps the cyclist have a comfortable ride. Cycling shorts tend to be on the long side and are always black. Both shorts and trousers are close fitting. Seat seams are the bane of the touring cyclist, so garments with high, stiff seams, like jeans, are best avoided. Tracksuits are fine for wear around the campsite, but rather baggy on the bike, and the right leg soon gets oil-smeared.

**Jerseys and jerkins** The essential feature here is that the pockets are on the back of the garment, not at the sides or front. If the pockets were placed there, the cyclist's leg action would either cause discomfort or quickly spill the pocket contents out on the road. For this reason, when I am not wearing 'proper' cycling clothing, I place my pocket contents (wallet, passport, keys, etc.) in a small Karrimor belt bag. Cycle jerkins are usually brightly coloured and sometimes have nylon wind- and waterproof front and shoulder facings, another winter boon. I usually manage quite well in a T-shirt once the day warms up, and since cycling is warm work, full-length zips are useful.

**Waterproofs** The traditional foul weather clothing for cyclists is a poncho and sou'wester, and this is still a useful and popular combination. Personally, I have opted for a waterproof Mistral suit in Gore-Tex fabric from Berghaus. Gore-Tex permits perspiration moisture to pass through the fabric, while excluding the larger rain drops. Since cycling in waterproofs is even hotter work, this is a useful feature. A neckerchief to keep the rain from running down the neck is also useful.

**Underwear** I work on the theory of one-on, one-off, and one-in-the-wash. I also avoid seams, or at least raised seams on the pants. Since cotton underwear washes easily and dries quickly, this wash-and-wear system can be maintained even on month-long tours. Cycling is grubby work and at the end of the day most cyclists will be pleasantly coated with a compound of perspiration and road dust, so washing the day's underwear in the campsite or hostel shower soon becomes a standard routine.

**Hat and gloves** Sooner or later you will fall off. Even at a slow speed, ungloved hands mean gravelled palms. Light, open-backed cycle gloves, perhaps with padded palms, are fine for summer, and some form of wrist-length gauntlet ideal for winter. A cap, with peak and ear flaps is also useful for the ears can get well nipped in the early morning, even in summer. Light cycling caps come in handy later in the day and help keep the hair clean, while those who wear a helmet are probably very wise.

**Bits and pieces** As a stroll round the shelves of any bike shop will soon reveal, there is virtually no end to the various knick-knacks that the cyclist can purchase. Please remember that even if you intend to use it you'll have to carry it, and if you don't use it, you have wasted your money, so buy only what you need. The essential extras are:
1. A pair of sunglasses, to be worn against the impact of insects as much as glare.
2. A tube of suncream.
3. A tube of lip salve.

**CAMPING EQUIPMENT** Let me make it clear that you don't usually *need* to camp or cook on a cycling tour. Meals can be eaten in cafes, nights passed in hotels and hostels. France is well provided with inexpensive hotels, auberges, *routier* cafes, and the shelters called gîtes d'étape. Avoiding camping will cut down on the weight you must carry, but it also puts the cost up and cuts down on the freedom and flexibility of the tour. I recommend that a certain amount of camping equipment be carried, at least a stove and a sleeping bag, just in case you get caught out.

The rule for all lightweight camping, and especially cycle-camping, is *take only what you need.* The two problems which must be overcome are those of weight and space, and only by applying this rule rigorously can the cycle-camper reduce the weight on the bike to an acceptable level and get everything in the panniers.

**The tent** The tent can be single-skinned, if the cyclist is certain that the tours will always be taken somewhere warm and fairly low. Anywhere high and chilly calls for a double-skinned, inner-and-fly tent. As a rule, a one-man tent takes a midget and a two-man takes one man, so get a two-man light-weight tent and then the vital parts of your equipment can be sheltered as well.

One suitable cyclist's tent is the Robert Saunders Jet-Packer, a double-skinned tent, with the option of a nylon or cotton inner (the cotton weighs 4oz more but is warmer), expanding poles, and fitted groundsheet. The two great advantages of this tent are the weight, 3½lb (1.5kg) and the packed size; when in the stuffsack it is a little more than 15in long, and thus fits easily on the carrier, ready for swift erecting, or final packing. Other tent manufacturers include Ultimate, Wintergear, and Phoenix. A bivvy-bag, in Gore-Tex, is a good alternative.

**Sleeping bag and mattress** A good night's sleep is essential. Here a mattress helps, and you will need a sleeping bag in

The Saunders Jet-Packer

hostels or gîtes d'étape. I use a self-inflating Thermarest mattress, available from any good camping shop and costing about £20. This has all the advantages of an air bed without the weight or bulk. For the same reason I use a Blacks Icelandic sleeping bag which is filled with down, very light and highly compressible.

Down can be a problem, for if it gets wet, the feathers matt and all insulation is lost. Wrap the bag in a plastic bag, even inside the pannier, to keep it dry.

**Cooking** There is a wide choice of stoves available. I stick to my old faithful SVEA 123, a petrol burner which weighs only 19oz, burns for well over an hour on one filling, and is only 5in high and 4in in diameter. For cooking I use Sigg pots and for that lightning lunchtime brew, a small Trangia kettle. A popular alternative, the Camping Gaz Globetrotter, is ideal for summer use and day tours, and Camping Gaz cartridges can be purchased all over France from camping shops or ironmongers (*quincaillerie*). Gaz cartridges are not permitted on aircraft.

Good, lightweight, camping equipment is expensive and not always easy to find. The would-be cycle-camper should seek out the address of a good outdoors shop in the Yellow Pages or write, enclosing £1 to *Field and Trek*, 22–25 Kings Road, Brentwood, Essex CM14 4ER, asking for a copy of their mail-order catalogue. This not only lists all the gear mentioned above, but also gives much useful advice on lightweight camping. A list of local camping shops can be found in the cycling or outdoor magazines (see Bibliography).

**Panniers** The rule here is that the equipment is carried on the bike and not on the rider, so no backpacks please. There are many makes of bike-bag and pannier available, Carradice, Eclipse and Pakit, to name but a few. Personally, I'm a Karrimor man. The latest range of Karrimor panniers, the Iberian range, have a storage capacity of 45 cubic litres, and currently cost around £26 a pair. With a handlebar bag for the small essential items, this combination takes all I need. It's only fair to add that since cycle-campers are an idiosyncratic crowd, there are wide differences of opinion on what to take and how to pack it. Everyone agrees on the need to take little as possible, and the lighter the better, but there is still much scope for debate as to how and where it should be carried.

Some swear they can get everything into a saddlebag, and for a weekend trip in summer so can I. Others go the whole hog, and can be seen wobbling through the traffic loaded with front and rear panniers, saddlebag and handlebar bag, but it looks like very hard work.

Ready for touring

Even on long trips I can get everything, and usually more than I need, into a pair of Karrimor panniers and a handlebar bag.

**SECURITY** As a precaution against all else failing, carry replacement-value insurance for both cycle and camping gear, and remember to extend the cover for touring abroad.

Security is the only real snag with cycletouring, for unless you enjoy staggering around, carrying two panniers, a bag, front wheel, and everything on the machine that isn't nailed down, you must chain up the machine *and* keep an eye on the luggage. If I intend to explore a town or cathedral, I begin by taking a coffee in some cafe and chatting to the owner or waiter. Then I ask if I can chain my machine to some part of the establishment. If someone else attempts to remove it they notice, and they usually offer some secure shelter. Try it.

Into the handlebar bag go the valuable and essential items, camera, film, passport, money, lock and chain. I *always* take the handlebar bag with me, even when crossing the pavement from the kerb to look in a shop window. I *always* chain the bike up, preferably to something solid. It's as well to have a rule about this, because one mistake in the wrong place and away goes bike and gear.

**LOADING** Having got all the clothing and equipment together, it must be packed in the panniers and loaded on the bike. Put the heavy items in the bottom, to get the weight as low as possible. Try to get the weight the same in each pannier. Have as little weight as possible in the handlebar bag. Fit the panniers to the machine, check they are secure and won't come off at the first bump, and then go for a short ride, choosing a route which includes the steepest local hill.

You will probably find, to your considerable consternation, that a loaded bike handles quite differently from the unladen machine. The frame flexes and wobbles alarmingly. Don't worry, you'll get used to it. When you get to that hill you will also get my point about 'Granny' gears. A few, short, fully-loaded trips like this before the main tour begins will get the cyclist tour-fit and able to handle the loaded machine competently.

**CYCLETOURING ORGANISATIONS**   There are a number of organisations and companies in the U.K. and in France, directly concerned with cycletouring. These concerns are mentioned in the book, but all British cycletourists should begin by joining the Cyclists Touring Club. The C.T.C. is over a hundred years old and has vast experience of cycletouring at home and abroad. The Club is organised around local clubs, or District Associations, which members usually join, and apart from Club runs and meetings, there is a bi-monthly magazine, *Cycletouring*, a C.T.C. handbook, and leaflets available on all aspects of cycling; so join now:

The Cyclists Touring Club
Cotterell House,
69 Meadrow,
Godalming, Surrey GU7 3HS.
Telephone: Godalming (04868) 7217.

Cycletouring organisations and sources of information specifically concerned with France are given in the next chapter.

**STARTING TO TOUR**   Once the cyclist has the machine and the equipment, the next logical step is to put the two together and go on a few tours. The cycletours in France described in this book can last anything from a week to a month, and no wise traveller sets off abroad on such trips without gaining at least a little previous experience here at home.

These one- or two-day tours will teach the cycletourist more than any amount of reading. They will teach *roadcraft*, and all the little tricks of riding a loaded bike on modern roads. The cyclist will discover that although the edge of the road may seem safer it can be littered with broken tarmac, potholes, glass and, in season, thorny hedge clippings. A pace that can be maintained will be discovered. It may be 10, 12 or 15 miles per hour, for hours on end, but it will be your pace, and with it you can calculate daily mileages.

In addition, the wise cyclist will obtain some of the titles listed in the bibliography and read up on bikes and cycletouring . . . it's all useful knowledge and scraps of knowledge can add up to an enjoyable tour.

**DISTANCES** After consulting with various experienced cyclists, and from my own travels, I recommend 80km (50 miles) a day as a good average for a cycling tour. Note the word average, for terrain, weather and fitness may dictate 30km on one day and 100km the next. I have also noticed considerable differences between the distance calculated on the map and the amount that appears on my kilo-mileometer, which is usually more. Those side trips and rides around the town all add up. The distances given for the tours in this book are calculations taken from maps and speedo readings, but the distance you, the tourist, will travel will vary from this according to how many corners are cut and how many diversions you make.

\* \* \*

All this touring experience is useful, indeed essential, before setting off across the Channel to start touring in France. The cycletourist is a traveller uncossetted by the assistance available to those on package trips, and the experience gained at home will come in very handy when, as will inevitably happen, things go wrong. With the right attitude, problems and the minor disasters—that inconvenient puncture, the train that never arrived—become part of the adventure, and anyway, you have to put up with them. The French have a very useful verb which they employ on such occasions, *se débrouiller*, which roughly translates as *to untangle* or get out of a difficulty. Cycletourists in France will learn how to *se débrouiller*, and as you will discover, it's all part of the fun of cycletouring in France.

# Chapter 2
# Touring in France
**'Dictum sapienti sat est.'**

France is the largest country in Western Europe, a vast, diverse, sprawling country, twice the size of the United Kingdom, spreading down from the Channel coast and the northern frontier with Belgium, south to the Mediterranean and the Pyrénées, east to the hills and mountains of the Alps, Vosges and Jura. Jutting west, out into the steep Atlantic stream, Brittany awaits the visitor, while just across the Channel lies the familiar country of Picardy and the Pas-de-Calais, and the rolling countryside of Normandy, a landscape often compared with that of Berkshire or Sussex, but also familiar, one might add, as our historic battlegrounds from the Hundred Years War to the more recent campaigns of 1914–18 and 1944. France is a country rich in history, scenery and variety. Much of it may seem familiar, for the histories of France and Britain have often intertwined, but the visitor who comes to France with an open mind and murmurs *Vive la différence* at least once a day, will have taken a major step towards discovering the full attractions of this beautiful country. France *is* different from Britain; not better, not worse, just different, and for the Francophiles among us, in this difference lies the great secret of its charm. The tours in this book are not just for those who enjoy cycling. They are for those who will find, by cycling, that they can get a closer, gentler, more enjoyable look at the diverse attractions of France. So let us begin.

**TERRAIN** As a glance at the topographic map (Fig. 7) will quickly reveal, France has a very varied terrain. The Alps and Pyrénées are mountains, the Jura, Vosges, Massif Central are extremely hilly, and only the forested Landes, which lie behind the coastline south of Bordeaux are truly flat, and for that reason somewhat dull. For the rest, the countryside is diverse and interesting, well supplied with minor roads and perfect for cycletouring. The hills tend to be less steep than those of Britain, but the climbs and descents often go on far longer.

**Fig. 7** The topography of France

Many minor roads are also scenic routes, providing fine views over the countryside. They are marked green on most maps and should be used whenever possible. Broadly speaking, the terrain grows wilder and more hilly as the traveller moves east and south, the colours of the countryside being influenced by the rainfall, green and soft to the west and north, changing to red and gold once the traveller crosses the Loire. The terrain is described in each of the following tours, and should be borne in mind when selecting a route to follow. Those with a highly-geared bike, or who hate hills, should avoid the Vosges or the more obvious Alps, while those who enjoy whirling across the high country can prospect happily in the Auvergne. Whatever you want is here, but study the contours closely.

**CLIMATE**  The cycletourist is exposed to the elements, and the generally warmer weather in France has to be taken into account when planning a tour. The chart on page 00 shows temperatures in different parts of France at various times of the year, but as a general rule I usually advise those who wish to be certain of good weather to head for somewhere south of the Loire, any time from Easter to October, although down there it can get very hot indeed.

Table 1  Average temperatures in France

| Average air temperatures °C | Jan Feb | Mar Apr | May Jun | Jul Aug | Sep Oct | Nov Dec |
|---|---|---|---|---|---|---|
| Paris-Ile-de-France | 5 | 11 | 15 | 19 | 14 | 5 |
| Alsace-Lorraine | 1 | 10 | 16 | 19 | 12 | 3 |
| Aquitaine | 7 | 13 | 16 | 19 | 17 | 9 |
| Auvergne | 2 | 11 | 14 | 18 | 12 | 3 |
| Brittany | 3 | 9 | 13 | 17 | 13 | 8 |
| Burgundy | 2 | 11 | 15 | 19 | 13 | 2 |
| Champagne-Ardenne | 2 | 10 | 14 | 18 | 13 | 4 |
| Corsica | 7 | 12 | 17 | 21 | 18 | 10 |
| Franche-Comté | 0 | 10 | 15 | 18 | 13 | 2 |
| Languedoc-Roussillon | 8 | 13 | 19 | 22 | 18 | 8 |
| Limousin | 3 | 10 | 14 | 18 | 13 | 4 |
| Midi-Pyrénées | 5 | 12 | 16 | 21 | 15 | 6 |
| Nord and Picardy | 3 | 9 | 14 | 17 | 12 | 3 |
| Poitou-Charentes | 5 | 10 | 14 | 18 | 13 | 5 |
| Provence | 8 | 13 | 19 | 24 | 18 | 10 |
| Riviera | 8 | 13 | 18 | 23 | 18 | 10 |
| Rhône valley | 1 | 11 | 16 | 20 | 14 | 6 |
| Savoy and Dauphiny Alps | −2 | 8 | 14 | 17 | 11 | 1 |
| Val de Loire-Centre | 3 | 11 | 14 | 19 | 13 | 6 |
| Western Loire | 6 | 11 | 15 | 19 | 14 | 6 |

Source: Direction de la Météorologie de France

The weather in Brittany, Normandy and the north of France tends to reflect that of Britain, although since the British Isles get the first brunt of the wet Atlantic westerly winds and relieve them of much of their moisture, even the most western provinces of France tend to be marginally drier and warmer than Britain. Brittany tends to be a showery province and the western Pyrénées, though far to the south, stay green thanks to the Atlantic winds.

Southern France has a warm Mediterranean climate, while that of the central provinces, Burgundy, the Auvergne, the eastern Alps and Rhône valley, has a 'Continental' climate, warm summers, cold winters, sharp frosts, snow on the high ground for most of the winter.

Crossing the high mountain passes (or cols) can be a chilly process and warm, windproof clothing may be necessary even on a summer morning. I have seen snow blocking the Col de Tourmalet in the Pyrénées as late as July. On balance though, France has good weather, and south of the Loire it can get tremendously hot. Cycling along in the summer heat, especially if the wind is blowing, will leech moisture from the body, so in those warmer climes the cyclist would be well advised to get up early, just after dawn, and get most of the day's distance completed in the morning, before the sun really beats down.

**THE FRENCH** One of the greatest assets of France, along with an agreeable climate and varied terrain, is the people. There are some 58 million French, a population roughly the same as that of the U.K. but even more diverse in origin. Within that umbrella term are Corsicans and Catalans, Normans, Picards, Basques, and many more, all French, all different. Although I realise that this may be a debatable point, let me state here that I like the French. In over 20 years of wandering about their country I have never found them less than friendly, kind, and certainly to the walker and cyclist, overwhelmingly helpful and hospitable. I could not say that they are the easiest people in the world, but the trick, if there is one, is to meet the French half-way. The French tend to be formal, so a handshake and a '*Bonjour*' should precede all discussion. It helps immensely if the visitor speaks, or at least tries to speak a little French, especially in the country districts where the visitor will be dragged from the saddle and offered a glass of wine on the slightest excuse if he or she seems to be agreeable and interesting.

The real secret seems to lie in the visitor's attitude. Those who go to France expecting trouble from waiters, taxi-drivers and porters, are almost sure to invite it by their prejudice. I expect that the people I meet will be helpful and friendly, and as a result they invariably are. Only last month, cycling in Picardy, one of our group crashed from his machine, buckling the front wheel and breaking five spokes. The local garage proprietor went out in his car to fetch him, and repaired the bike in less than an hour; this was on a Sunday afternoon. An hotel proprietor, on the same trip, although overwhelmed by a wedding party in his restaurant, nevertheless cooked us a good meal, served· it to us in our rooms, and gave us the run of the kitchen to fetch more wine. Neither grumbled about it all being too much trouble.

The cycletourist will need help from time to time, from railway clerks, bike-shop owners, campsite proprietors and the like. A big smile and a *'Pouvez-vous m'aider?'* ('can you help me?') will go a long way towards getting it.

**Fig. 8** The *Départements* of France

**ADMINISTRATION** It will help if the visitor has some idea of how France works. Even the French will admit that France is a highly centralised country, where all the roads lead to Paris. France is governed on a parliamentary system, currently by a Socialist coalition, administered on a three-tier system, the *commune*, the *département*, and the region or province. Of these the most important is the *département*.

There are 95 *départements* in France (Fig. 8) usually named after the principal local river; Seine-Maritime, Haute Loire, Cher, Yonne, and so on. The *départements* were established by Napoleon, who, to ensure that the People would be heard, decreed that no *département* should be so big that a resident from the furthest fringe could not get to the administrative capital and home again, on horseback, in one day. Although the system is currently under review, each *département* is administered by a senior civil servant, the *préfect*, who is appointed by and reports to the President of the Republic.

Over the last couple of decades these *départements* have been grouped into larger administrative units or regions, some based on the ancient French provinces of the *ancien régime*, Normandy, Burgundy, Brittany, Languedoc and so on, which existed before the French Revolution of 1789. Others are entirely modern, artificial creations, like Pays de la Loire or Western France, and designed to link predominately agricultural areas with industrial centres, to their mutual support and advantage. There are 23 such regions in Metropolitan France and the cycle tours in this book are largely based upon that provincial framework.

## SERVICES IN FRANCE

**Roads** The cyclist in France will be most concerned with the road. France has a good motorway (*autoroute*) network of toll roads from which cyclists are banned, and a vast number of other roads so that, compared with the U.K., their roads often seem empty. The *Routes Nationales* or 'N' roads, are excellent, but cyclists should, whenever possible, avoid these and use the quieter *départemental* or 'D' roads and scenic routes. Road numbers seem to change continually, as 'D' roads become 'N' and vice-versa, which can be confusing, so good map reading is helpful. Cycle tracks are increasing in number, especially in urban areas, and where they exist their use is mandatory. All traffic travels on the right. Note that traffic on roundabouts now has priority over traffic entering them and that in towns traffic coming from the right has priority (*Priorité à droite*). Motorists are obliged to sound their horns at cyclists and give them a wide berth. Cyclists are expected to ride single file and keep to the right.

**Cycle regulations** Cycles can be imported free into France if for personal use. They must be in good working order and have a warning system (bell or horn), lights, and a reflector. French cyclists usually label their machines with their name, address and even their blood group.

**Telephones** The French telephone service is rapidly improving, and direct dial call boxes can be found everywhere. To dial Britain from France, the visitor:

(a) dials 19 for an international line (a high-pitched note)
    – then –
(b) 44
    – and –
(c) the U.K. area code, (minus the 0)
    – and –
(d) then the number.

For example: To dial a London number 123 4567 the complete dialling code is 19-44-1-123-4567. To dial France from the U.K. the codes are 010 (for an international line), then 33, followed by the area code, for example: 7 for Lyon, and then the local number.

The *interdépartemental* code in France is 16. For example, anyone in Normandy phoning from, say, the Orne *département* to book a room or a campsite in the *département* of Calvados, must prefix the French area code for Calvados (31) with 16.

The Police code is 17, the Operator 13, Directory enquiries 12. A telephone directory in France is called a *Bottin*.

**Post Offices** Post Offices or P.T.T. (for *Poste, Telephone, Tele-graphe*) can be found in all French towns and most villages. Look for the P.T.T. sign. *Post Restante* facilities are available in towns, and mail addressed c/o *Poste Restante/Poste Centrale* can be collected for a small fee at main post offices. If they say they don't have any mail and you are *sure* it is there, men could try asking the staff to check again under Esq. (for Esquire).

**Passports and documentation** British visitors to France need a valid British passport or a British Visitor's Passport (valid for one year). Carry your passport with you at all times. No visas are necessary, but those using campsites or hostels may find an International Camping Carnet useful. These can be obtained through the Camping Club of Great Britain and Northern Ireland, 11 Lower Grosvenor Place, London SW1 (Tel: 01-818 1012) or the C.T.C. Membership of both organisations is recommended to cycle-campers.

Campsite proprietors may ask for some form of identification and retain it for the duration of the camper's stay. Those without a Carnet may be asked to hand over their passport, which is never a good idea. I should add though that except on T.C.F. (Touring Club de France) sites, I have never been asked for my Carnet. Should the visitor lose his passport or money, or get into legal difficulties, the British Embassy is at 35 Rue du St. Honoré, Paris. There are now very few British Consulates in France, and they are usually in ports, but their addresses can be found in the *Bottin*.

**Metrication**   The wise tourist in France should start to think in metric terms as soon as possible, especially over distances. A kilometre is five-eighths of a mile (5 furlongs), so:

$$8km = 5 \text{ miles}$$
$$24km = 15 \text{ miles}$$
$$80km = 50 \text{ miles}$$

To convert kilometres back into miles, divide by eight and multiply by five, so:

$$\frac{40km}{8} \times 5 = 25 \text{ miles}$$

Other useful measurements are:

$$1kg = 2.2lb$$
$$500g = 1lb \text{ (approx)}$$
$$250g = .5lb$$
$$1l = 1.75 \text{ pints}$$

France works on the Centigrade (Celcius) temperature scale. To convert Centigrade to Fahrenheit, apply the following formula:
temperature $°C \times 2 - 10\% + 32 = $ temperature $°F$
$16°C \times 2 = 32 - 3 = 29° + 32 = 61°F$
— and so $16°C = 61°F$ . . . comfortably warm.

**Time**   France works on the 24-hour clock, so 7.00 p.m. is 1900. Note that for much of the year France is one hour ahead of Britain, so bear this in mind when checking timetables.

**Medical services**   The French have a national health service similar to that of Britain, with the significant difference that patients first pay for all or part of the treatment and then reclaim the cost from the Government. The cost of a consultation is currently around 65 francs, (£6). British visitors to France can use this service if they first obtain a Form No. E111, obtainable from the local D.H.S.S. office. This will enable you to reclaim about 80 per cent of medical costs incurred. Apply for Form No. E111 well in advance of the tour, as getting this form can take some time. This concession is not available to the self-employed or the unemployed. French doctors (*le médecin*) and hospitals are very good and French chemists (*pharmacies*) are obliged to give First Aid treatment, so if you fall and graze a knee, apply for help to the local *pharmacie*. There is a small charge for this service, so better still, carry a First Aid kit and know how to use it.

**Banks and currency** The French franc is divided into 100 centimes. Coins are available for 5, 10, 20 and 50 centimes and 1, 2, 5 and 10 francs. Notes are available for 1, 10, 20, 50, 100, 200, 500 and 1000 francs. Banks are open between 0900 and 1200, and from 1400 to 1600 on weekdays, and closed at weekends and public holidays. France has 11 public holidays per year, so be sure the banks are open before you run out of cash.

**Cheques and credit cards** Diners, American Express, Visa and other credit cards are accepted in France, but some cash and traveller's cheques are advisable. Most French banks on the Eurocheque system and displaying the EC symbol, will cash U.K. cheques of up to £50 in value providing they are supported by the Eurocheque card. This is *not* the standard U.K. cheque card, but a special card obtainable from any U.K. High Street bank. Money, cheques and credit cards should be kept securely on the person at all times, but not all together in the same bag, wallet or pocket.

**ACCOMMODATION** France has a wide range of accommodation of all styles and prices, from five-star luxury hotels with carpet on the walls to small farm campsites with the most limited facilities. So finding somewhere to stay is usually the least of the traveller's problems outside the high season. In the high season periods, around Easter and July/August, it would pay the traveller to ring ahead and book, or seek somewhere to stay by the early evening. Those on cycle-camping trips will have no difficulty finding a pitch, for a small tent will fit in somewhere, even on a crowded site, while pitches on a farm site or behind a hedge are always an alternative option.

Places which are full usually display a *complet* sign, but it is still worth asking if space or rooms are available as they may simply have forgotten to take it down from the night before.

**Hotels** Hotels in France are graded from five-star 'luxury' down to no-star 'adequate'. The hotelier will expect the visitor to inspect the room before taking it. Room prices include tax and service but no breakfast and, a useful tip, the pillows are usually in the wardrobe. The Michelin Red Guide, an annual publication, is a most useful book, and the prices given in the

Michelin will be those charged by the hotel during that year. Prices are also displayed in the reception area and behind the room door.

Another useful hotel guide is the annual *Guide des Logis et Auberges de France*, obtainable free from the French Government Tourist Office (F.G.T.O.), 178 Piccadilly, London, and published in March each year. This lists over 5000 family-owned hotels in provincial France, often inexpensive and offering local dishes at reasonable prices, and I recommend them to the reader. When I am not camping I, personally, prefer to stay in Logis hotels.

**Youth hostels**  France is not over supplied with youth hostels and the standard overall cannot be compared with that of youth hostels in England. A list of addresses can be obtained from the Y.H.A., 14 Southampton Street, London WC2 E7HY, Tel: 01-836 8541, or from the Fédèration Unie des Auberges de la Jeunesse, 6 Rue Mesnil, 75116 Paris.

**Gîtes d'Etape**  If youth hostels are not widely available, especially in the country districts where they would be most useful, France is increasingly covered with hostels, designed for walkers and cyclists and known as *gîte d'étape*. These are normally found in the smaller villages or on large farms where outbuildings and barns have been equipped with showers, bunks and stoves, and offer simple but perfectly adequate accommodation, currently for less than F20 a night. Gîtes are usually unmanned and it may be necessary to obtain the key from the farm or a nearby cafe, but some do have *guardiens* who will cook meals. A list of gîtes d'étape can be obtained from local *Syndicat d'Initiatives* or Regional Tourist Boards or those organisations such as A.B.R.I. in Brittany, or Chamina in the Massif Central, which specialise in outdoor activities (see page 60).

**Campsites**  France has thousands of campsites and, as with hotels, their standards are described by a star system. A four-star site will have a pool, maybe two, shops, entertainment, and lots of tents. A small *camping a la fèrme* (farm camping) site may only have space for six tents and a cold-water tap, so the choice is wide. Average charges are modest, at around F.10 a night, and most 2–3 star sites will have hot showers and washing facilities available. A list of regional 'campings' can be obtained from the F.G.T.O. or from the local Syndicat d'Initiative. In summer it is usually advisable to arrive early, or ring ahead and book a pitch, but a small cycle-camping tent will usually fit in somewhere, even when the sign on the gate says

'*Complet*'. A big smile and a '*J'ai seulement une petite tente*' will often melt the *guardien*'s heart.

**Food and drink** One of the great and undisputed pleasures of France is the eating. The cuisine of France is world famous, and rightly so, for you will eat better, and at lower cost, in France than anywhere else in the world. The great dishes of France come from such provincial areas as Normandy, Burgundy and the Périgord, but as a rule the cooking is of a high standard everywhere and well suited to the local wines, which France can offer in abundance. Apart from Burgundy, Bordeaux and Beaujolais, think of the Rhône, Muscadet, Côtes du Roussillon, Sancerre, Chinon . . . ah!

A great big meal with wine in the middle of the day will simply stop a cyclist in his tracks and is best avoided. I begin with breakfast, have an early picnic lunch and devote the evening to seeking out the best local restaurant for a good meal. The usual French breakfast of a roll and coffee can be too insubstantial for cycling, so eating a bar of chocolate as well can help to stave off the dreaded 'bonk', that dire feeling when all the cyclist's energy just fades away. I have a picnic lunch early, around twelve o'clock, safely out of the way at the time when the roads are crowded with French motorists rushing home for lunch, their minds other than on their driving.

This picnic usually sets me up for the rest of the day. Bread can be found in a *boulangèrie*, and all the other ingredients for a good picnic, cheese, ham, fruit, a bottle of wine, from an *épicerie* or a self-service grocer (*alimentation*). If you need water for a brew, cemeteries are marked on maps and usually contain a tap. Do not drink water marked '*Eau non potable*'.

**INFORMATION ON GETTING TO FRANCE** Any good trip is founded on up-to-the-minute, accurate information. This presents any author with a problem for all information tends to date, and those planning a tour to France are therefore advised to seek up-to-date information from as wide a choice of informants as possible.

The basic source of information on France is: The French Government Tourist Office, 178 Piccadilly, London W1V 0AL; tel: 01-491 7622. Write, call, or better still, visit, with a list of your requirements well in advance of the departure date. If writing for information enclose at least 50p in stamps on a large self-addressed envelope.

For rail information apply to the nearest British Rail Information Office, which can be located at the nearest main railway station, or, for details on rail travel inside France contact: French Rail, 178 Piccadilly, London W1V 0AL; tel: 01-493 4451/

2. I have found this organisation most helpful in providing reliable information on those trains in France which carry cycles, but even so, I always re-check the information on the spot.

Information on air travel must be obtained from the airlines, not from High Street travel agents. The principal airlines are Air France, British Airways and Dan-Air. *Air France* can be contacted at (1) Georgian House, 69 Boston Manor Road, Brentford, Middx; all enquiries tel: 01-568 4411; or (2) 158 New Bond Street, London W1Y 0AY; enquiries, tel: 01-499 8611, reservations tel: 01-499 9511; or (3) London (Heathrow) Airport, passenger and general cargo enquiries: 01-759 3211; Manchester Airport tel: (061 489) 3303. *British Airways* London (Heathrow) enquiries tel: 01-759 2525 or 01-759 3131; London (Gatwick) tel: (0293) 31299; Manchester: enquiries tel: (061 437) 5277. *Dan-Air* 36–38 New Broad Street, London EC2M 1NH; all enquiries Tel: 01-638 1747; London (Gatwick) all enquiries tel: (0293) 513631; Manchester all enquiries tel: (061 437) 5277.

If the query concerns your cycle ask for 'passenger handling' or if they prove vague ask for 'baggage handling'. State your query and condition as precisely as possible. If your cycle is actually a tandem or a tricycle say so, for airlines won't carry tricycles; tandems, though longer than normal bikes, are still usually accepted.

If the airline does not *usually* carry cycles, ask that the check-in desk be advised that you are taking one. It all saves dramas on the day.

\* \* \*

Before we proceed to look at trip planning in detail, let me stress again that good trips are based on good information. This, in turn, is based on the traveller asking specific questions which will elicit specific, unequivocal replies. Beware of such phrases as, 'It *should* be all right . . . it *may* be possible . . . I *think* so'. Press until you get a specific answer, and even then, check it. Things will still go wrong, but then that is all part of the game, and if you have the correct attitude to independent travel, also part of the fun.

**TRAVELLING TO FRANCE** The easiest and least troublesome way of travelling to France is to do as much as possible of the journey on the bike, riding to the ferry terminal or airport and only relying on others for the actual passage across the Channel by sea or air. However, since time is usually limited, this is rarely possible, and some form of public transport has to be employed.

**Air travel** Air travel, if the most expensive, is also the simplest. There are direct, scheduled flights to many parts of France by Air France, British Airways, Dan-Air, Brymon, and several other airlines. Air-Inter is the French internal airline. It is possible to fly direct from the U.K. to Nice, Paris, Bordeaux, Marseilles, Lyon, Montpellier, Perpignan, Strasbourg, Ajaccio, and a number of other airports. Charter airlines carry package holidaymakers to even smaller destinations. Information on which airline goes where can be obtained from High Street travel agents or the F.G.T.O. Detailed enquiries can then be made directly to the airline.

Cycles travel by air as part of the baggage allowance, normally 20kg (44lb) and the panniers or saddlebags can go as hand luggage in the cabin. It is as well to check with the airline that they will carry cycles, but even charter airlines are open to suggestions in the low season months. Cycles do not need to be bagged or boxed but the cyclist should arrive at the airport early, at least an hour before the advertised check-in time, to argue out any problems and avoid the queue. Remove all loose items, handlebar bag, panniers, pump, bottles etc., and keep a few tools to hand for dismantling parts of the machine.

The handlebars must be turned parallel with the top tube, and the pedals must be removed. Check before arriving at the airport that they will come off easily, remembering that the left-hand pedal has a left-hand thread. It *may* be necessary to remove the front wheel, which is when those quick release hubs come in handy, and some airlines insist that the tyres are deflated. Try to avoid this, for most baggage holds are now pressurised so deflation is not necessary and if the cycle is wheeled about with flat tyres the innertubes may be punctured. Carry straps or two short lengths of shock-cord to fasten the front wheel to the frame, and a little rubber padding or cardboard snapped around the *dérailleur* with a rubber band can protect the mechanism. A block of wood or an axle-bolt across the front forks can stop them being crushed.

Most airlines are now well used to bikes and the system is simple and effective. Air travel can be expensive, but it is also quick, and if the traveller adds in the time and convenience gained in return, then buying an air ticket may be well worth the extra money.

**Rail travel to France** The ports most convenient for France lie in the south and south-east of Britain so, unless you live in the south of England, it will usually be necessary to take the cycle to the port by rail. Rail travel with a cycle is a complex and constantly changing situation, and one best tackled step by step.

It is said to be possible to send your bike ahead to France *or* take it with you, as accompanied baggage. This is true, up to a point, but there are snags, and the major snag is inter-station transfers. Sending the bike ahead cannot be recommended, since it takes time, up to five days from London to Paris, separates the cyclist from the machine, and seems in practice to be a very hit or miss affair.

It is better, therefore, to take the cycle with you, but here too there are snags. British Rail regularly produces leaflets outlining the current position, which is sure to change, but broadly speaking the current situation is as follows:

1. Cycles are carried, free, subject to space being available, on all routes not operated by Inter-City 125's, and outside peak travel hours in main suburban areas. The cyclist puts the bike in the guard's van and takes it out again on arriving at the destination.
2. On other routes cycles may be carried subject to space being available at a charge which may vary from 70p for a reservation up to a maximum of £3 for a single journey.
3. Cycles *will* be carried, subject to space being available, on certain 125's, outside peak hours.

The actual situation as rendered in leaflets is much more complex and the effect of studying the problem is usually a headache and a sense of frustration. The answer though is simple. Cyclists wishing to get to a certain port or airport by a certain time should go to their nearest British Rail Information Office and ask the specific question, *'How do I get myself and my bike to Dover (or Newhaven or Portsmouth) in time to catch the ferry next Tuesday?'*

Faced with such a specific request, the Information Officers, usually friendly folk, will come up with a specific answer. For examples: to get to Portsmouth or Southampton, I first ride to Reading, which is 15 miles away from my home. There I take a train for Guildford. This train has a guard's van, into which I personally place the bike. At Guildford I wait for a train to Portsmouth, and from there the ferry terminals at Portsmouth and Southampton are within easy reach. Even so, this takes several hours and the time must be carefully calculated. To get to Ramsgate or Dover, I take a train from Maidenhead to Paddington, ride across to Victoria or Charing Cross, and then book the cycle for Dover Harbour, putting the cycle on the train myself.

The secret of rail travel is to obtain information well ahead of time, remembering the general exclusions, and then tackle the journey in stages. Do not book the cycle straight through, especially if this involves a change of station. Book each section separately, and do the linking rides, station to station, port to station, independently.

Three final tips. Firstly, when you have got the information from the British Rail Information Officer, ask him to write it out for you, preferably on British Rail notepaper. Remember to be specific. If, 'How can I and my bike get to . . .' actually means, '. . . my bike, myself and thirty-two other cyclists,' this can alter things. It's all subject to space, remember. However, that written note may come in handy if the train guard is reluctant to carry your cycle. Rules regarding cycles are constantly changing, so the guard may not be up-to-date. A little glamour can help, so if in reply to the hostile, 'And where do you think you're going with that then?' you can reply, 'the Pyrénées' or 'Saint Tropez', it may prove more effective in attracting help than 'Paddington'. Secondly, remembering space availability, don't travel on the last available train, allow time for error. Thirdly, remember there is usually a town station *and* a harbour station, and you will want the harbour station – or, if abroad, the *gare-maritime.*

**Car racks** If some kind soul can be talked into doing the driving, or you want to drive out to an area and tour from there, then transporting the bike by car to the port or to France can be an excellent idea.

Cycles can often be carried in the boot or transported on specially designed cycle roof-racks, or on rear-mounted racks attached to the boot. On balance I prefer the roof-rack, provided the driver remembers the cycle is up there when driving onto a low ferry deck or under a bridge, into stable yards, and the like. Chain cycles to the roof-rack for added security, and remove them completely overnight. It's worth mentioning that my car has been broken into three times in France, and I fear those foreign number plates draw thieves like a magnet. If the car has to be left for extended periods, find a secure spot, in a hotel or locked garage.

**Ferries to France** There are various ferries running to France from Ramsgate, Dover, Folkestone, Newhaven, Portsmouth, Southampton, Weymouth and Plymouth. These ferries arrive at Dunkirk, Calais, Boulogne, Dieppe, Le Havre, Cherbourg, St-Malo and Roscoff, and soon, perhaps Caen.

On most ferries and hovercraft, other than Brittany Ferries, cycles travel free. The cyclist rides or wheels the cycle onto the car deck, secures the machine with shock-cord to some convenient bulkhead, and retires to the bar. P & O Ferries even supply handy lengths of rope for lashing the cycle into place. It's all very painless and highly efficient. The ferry companies include Sealink, P & O Ferries, Townsend Thorenson, Sally Line, Hoverspeed, and Brittany Ferries, and full details on their various sailings, routes and times can be obtained from any High Street travel agent. Crossing times vary from less than an hour for Dover-Calais on the hovercraft, to all night on the route from Portsmouth to St. Malo. There are no Customs difficulties on bringing a cycle into France and the cyclist can be riding out of the port a few moments after docking. He or she should be aware of French road signs (see Fig. 9).

**Security** Cycle thefts are all too common, even in Britain, but can be an absolute disaster if a cycle is stolen in France. The price of security is eternal vigilance. Never let the cycle out of your sight unless it is locked up in a garage, your hotel room, a left-luggage office, or in the hands of a friendly local. In addition, chain it securely to some immovable object, and remove everything that isn't nailed down. Good locks, like the Kryptonite and Citadel will resist even well-equipped thieves, but the best security is to *keep the cycle in sight*.

**Fig. 9**

**Insurance** Adequate insurance is essential, and it should cover the cyclist, his machine, money and luggage against theft, loss, third party cover, injury or damage. Insurance for abroad can often be added to a current policy but be sure that any existing cycle insurance is valid for trips overseas. If not, obtain the necessary extension to the policy, or take out fresh insurance. A number of companies specialise in cycling insurance, and insurance is available at reduced rates, as one of many benefits available, to C.T.C. members.

**Police** Please note that if you are robbed of cycle, equipment or money, you *must* report the fact to the French police and get a form from them recording the event, and the items lost. Without this as proof of theft it is most unlikely that any insurance company will entertain your claim.

**TRAIN TRAVEL IN FRANCE** Once in France, it is still necessary to get to the starting point for the tour and although the French are enthusiastic cyclists, rail travel with a cycle in France is just as problematic as in Britain. The first point of contact for information on rail travel in France is the French Rail (S.N.C.F.) office in Piccadilly, London. As a rule, cycles travelling as unaccompanied baggage in France, can take between two and five days to arrive at their destination, whatever assurances are given by the S.N.C.F. clerks to the contrary. Cycles are not carried on high speed expresses or the recently introduced T.G.V. (*Trains Grands-Vitesse*) which operate like Inter-City.

As France is a centralised country, most train routes lead to or from Paris, so the cyclist heading for the South will usually need to go via Paris, and here the same rule regarding terminals applies. Make the journey one stage at a time. Book the cycle to the Paris station, Gare-de-Nord or St-Lazare, collect it at the other end, and then ride it across Paris to the next terminal, Gare-de-Lyon or Gare d'Austerlitz, and rebook it from there to the final destination. It is not always possible or even convenient to travel on the same train as your cycle. Only the tourist can decide whether it is more convenient to send the cycle on ahead and follow a day after, or go ahead and hope that the cycle will swiftly follow, but anyone parted from their machine must anticipate a delay of at least a day or two before they are united. Personally, I prefer to see the bike off on the train and follow after it. That way I know it has gone, and I hope will be waiting at the other end . . . On the return trip, remember to book and label the cycle for the *Gare-maritime* of your departure port, or it may go to the central station.

**Fig. 10** The French Railway System.

Now for the details. The current situation is as follows: Cycles can be taken as hand luggage on some 2000 French trains each day. The baggage office or ticket office will supply a wire-on label, which must be filled in and attached to the machine. The cyclist is responsible for putting the bike in the guard's van (*le fourgon*), securing it safely, and unloading it at the destination. Many such trains have special cycle waggons, and this service is free. These trains are coded nos. 39 or 40 in French Rail timetables, but not always, alas, on those conveniently displayed as posters at the railway stations. This code does appear in the regional timetable books held by the information offices at main terminals, so the cyclist must enquire there, as and when necesary.

Table 2 A French rail timetable

| Identification du train | | 8171 autorail | 8173 autorail |
|---|---|---|---|
| Prestations | places assises particularités | 1.2 [40] | 1.2 [40] |
| km | | | |
| 0 PERPIGNAN | | 6.00 | 8.02 |
| 8 Le Soler | | 6.08 | 8.10 |
| 13 St-Feliu-d'Avail | | | |
| 17 Millas | | 6.16 | 8.18 |
| 23 Ille-sur-Têt | | 6.23 | 8.25 |
| 26 Bouleternère | | | |
| 31 Vinça | | 6.33 | 8.35 |
| 40 Prades-Molitg-les-Bains | | 6.45 | 8.45 |
| 44 Ria | | 6.49 | 8.49 |
| 46 VILLEFRANCHE-VERNET-LES-BAINS | | 6.53 | 8.53 |

[40] Train acheminant gratuitement les bicyclettes en bagage à main.

Note that from September 1983, an illustration 🚲 will replace the numeral 40 or 39.

**Unaccompanied cycles** These must be checked in at the baggage office an hour before train time. Stay around to see that the bike is put on the platform and, if possible, on the train. It can be collected from the *livraison* at the other end half-an-hour after arrival. A number of stations are now offering cycle boxes to protect the machine, as a free service, and separate transit insurance is available and worth having.

**Hiring cycles** If your cycle has been swallowed up by the system, you can while away the waiting time by hiring a machine for a local tour. Touring cycles, 10-speed, mixte or gents, or sit-up-and-beg machines, are available from nearly 200 stations. A typical hire price is around £2 per day for a 10-speed machine.

It's only fair to stress at this point that in practice I have had no real trouble travelling to, from, and around France with my bike. I know the situation is as outlined here and I can allow for it. It would be very nice if my bike and I could travel together on any train whenever necessary, but this, alas, isn't always possible. Nor is it possible or wise for me to state categorically here what will happen to the cyclist and his machine over the next few years on some particular run. The above is the current, general situation. In practice there is no real problem, but delays can be anticipated. Check with the British or French Rail offices in London and as you go, book in stages and have patience. It will all come out right in the end . . . well, usually!

**Composter** Before boarding any French train, make certain that your ticket has been stamped or 'composted'. Orange *composter* machines stand at every platform (*quai*) entrance; insert the ticket into a slot, and it will be duly stamped. Failure to do so may result in the traveller having to pay the full fare again, when the ticket inspector comes round.

**COACH TRAVEL** Coach travel is possible even with a cycle, provided the driver can be convinced that the cycle can be disassembled and will not take up too much room in the luggage hold. It is always worth asking anyway. Some country buses will carry cycles on the roof, otherwise they go on the lower luggage compartments. Bus route information can be found from tourist boards and Syndicates d'Initiative, but there are few long-distance bus services in France; most country bus services operate within the *département*. A coach is a *bus*, a bus is a *car*, a ferry or airport shuttle bus is a *navette*.

\* \* \*

On the basis of this general information, the cycletourist can begin to plan his or her particular tour. Planning a tour takes time, but this planning should be regarded as an essential and enjoyable part of the trip, not as a time wasting chore. Plan well, and you will travel well.

**PLANNING A TOUR** The secret of a successful tour is adequate and accurate preplanning. All likely sources of information should be contacted, so that correct, up-to-date and (above all) reliable information can be obtained covering the following points:
1. Information on the touring area, terrain, weather.
2. Getting from home to U.K. port or airport, and home afterwards, including costs.
3. Crossing to France and back: how?
4. Internal French travel: Daily stages—itinerary.
5. Accommodation, campsites, gîtes d'étape.
6. Currency, traveller's cheques, passport, Eurocheque card.
7. Maps and guides, phrase book, dictionary.
8. Insurance, medical.
9. Prepare packing list relevant to tour (see Tour 20).

10. Getting bikes serviced and riders tour fit before the start.
    Gearing. Spares.

This list could be expanded almost endlessly, but it gives the general idea.

**Maps and guides** Apart from a good plan you need good maps, and there is a wide choice available. The C.T.C. recommend the Michelin yellow maps, scale 1/200,000, 1cm:2km *avec relief*, as the best for the cycletourist. These maps show all the roads in detail and outline the 'scenic routes', those well worth travelling for the beauty of the view, in green. These yellow maps are very useful for picking your way across the country on minor roads, and give a great deal of other information, indicating hills and gradients. The recently introduced 1/200,000 *regional* Michelin maps are very good on longer tours.

Personally, for planning a tour, I prefer the 1:250,000 IGN (Institut Géographique National) red Carte Touristique. This scale, 1cm:2.5km is slightly smaller than the yellow Michelin but, as the name implies, they are touring maps; they show the sites and places of interest, the castles and abbeys and all the things one might otherwise miss. Allied to a good guide book, and one or two of the yellows, they give the tourist all the background to the area and add to the interest of the tour. There are twenty maps in this IGN series and I used these to plan the tours in this book. Other tourists prefer the IGN 1/100,000 green Carte Touristique, a large and useful scale, with plenty of detail.

The Michelin red maps nos. 998 France Nord, and 999 France Sud, scale 1cm:10km are useful for more general planning and finding a route to the start of the tour.

Useful guidebooks, worth culling for information, are the annual Michelin Guide, the Guide des Logis de France, the Collins Companion Guide series, or the Michelin Green Guides. A full list is given in the bibliography. A good selection of maps and guides can be obtained from the C.T.C., Stanfords Map Shop in Long Acre, London, or the U.K. agents for the IGN, McCarta Ltd., 122 Kings Cross Road, London WC1X 9DS; tel: 01-278 8278, who operate a mail-order service.

Two final and most useful books are a phrase book, and a pocket dictionary. The Collins *Gem Dictionary* is ideal. A list of words and phrases relevant to cycletouring is given in the appendices and can be learned or copied into a notebook.

**SOURCES OF INFORMATION** A number of sources are given in the appendices, or on previous pages, but anyone planning a visit to France should begin by obtaining all the information possible from the French Government Tourist Office

(FGTO) in London, or one of the regional tourist offices. C.T.C. members will get much good advice from their club. More detailed advice can also be obtained from a number of French organisations which are particularly concerned with open-air activities. The principal organisation for cycletourists in France is the Fédération Française de Cyclotourisme, 8 Rue Jean Marie Jego, 75013 Paris; tel: (1) 580 30 21. Their office is open Monday–Saturday inclusive, 10.00–18.00 hr.

Another useful organisation is the Touring Club de France (T.C.F.), 65 Avenue de la Grande Armée, 75782 Paris Cédex 16, tel: (1) 553 39 59 or 727 89 89.

Apart from these two, the F.G.T.O., the regional tourist offices and the outdoor organisations, every French town and village of any size will have a tourist office, or Syndicat d'Initiative, where local information can be obtained. Unfortunately these offices are not always open, but if they are, a visit can be rewarding. If you are going to be in Paris, it is worth knowing that the Avenue de la Grande Armée, beyond the Arc de Triomphe, is full of cycle shops.

**Regional outdoor organisations** These organisations will be able to provide you with much useful information.
*Nord—pas-de-Calais*: F.R.A.R. (Fédération Regionale des Associations de Randonnée), 157 Boulevard de la Liberté, 59000 Lille; tel: (20) 57 35 23. *Picardy*: A.G.E.P. (Association des gîtes d'étape de Picardie), B.P. 0342, 80003 Amiens Cédex; tel: (22) 95 65 00. *Brittany*: A.B.R.I. (Association Bretonne Relais et Itinéraires), 3 Rue des Portes Mordelaises; tel: (99) 79 36 26. *Massif Central*: Chamina (Association pour le développement de la Randonnée pédestre dans le Massif Central), 5 Rue Pierre le Vénérable, 63000 Clermont-Ferrand; tel: (73) 92 82 60. *Franche-Comté*: G.T.J. (Grande Traversée du Jura) Comité Regional de Tourisme, 1 Place de la Première Armée, 25041 Besançon; tel: (81) 80 92 55. *Alpes*: G.T.A. (Grande Traversée des Alpes), Maison due Tourisme, 14 Rue de la Republique—B.P. 227, 38019 Grenoble Cedex; tel: (76) 54 34 36. *Languedoc-Roussillon et Cévennes*: A.T.R. (Association de Tourisme de Randonnée Languedoc-Roussillon), 12 Rue Foch, 34000 Montpellier; tel: (67) 60 55 42. *Midi-Pyrénées*: C.O.R.A.M.I.P. (Comité de Randonnée Midi-Pyrénées), 3 Rue de l'Esquile, 31000 Toulouse; tel: (61) 21 41 54.

A sample enquiry letter in French and English is given in Appendix 1. When writing to any organisation in France, enclose a large self-addressed envelope *and* an International Reply Coupon for at least 50p. This can be obtained from any U.K. post office.

Do not, however, restrict your researches to official sources, at home or abroad. Go to the library and get out guidebooks. Read articles in the appropriate magazines. If you are planning something obscure, write to the magazine's letter page and request information from other readers. The more you know about the area you are touring, the more you will enjoy the tour.

**Notebook**  With weight the main enemy, no cyclist would take off for France on a cycle loaded with books, maps and similar impedimenta. When planning the tour, first buy a notebook and jot down the relevant information for that tour, extracting it from numerous guides and informative leaflets. I have some 30 such notebooks covering the tours made for this book, and they make a useful record. Into the notebook goes all the information needed, culled from the heavier sources of reference.

**Kit and clothing**  One of the lists that should be prepared early, is the one covering kit and clothing. It is important to take all that you need, and nothing more, for let it be stressed again, extra weight is a burden to rider and machine. A full list of appropriate clothing is given in Tour 20 (and see pp 30–32), though thought must be given to the terrain and the time of year. Warm clothing can be useful even in summer, on mountain tours.

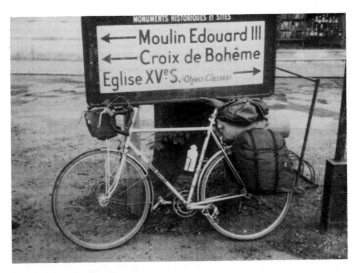

Loaded for the Road

A party should try and carry as many items of kit as possible on a group basis. Stove, fuel, tent (split into inner and fly), food, water, tools, repair outfit, even tyres can be carried on a group basis. Note also that many items can be bought freely in France. Such items as food and Camping Gaz cartridges are widely available and need not be carried in bulk. There is no need for everyone to carry a complete kit, and weight shared is weight reduced. It does mean though, that the group must stay together.

Once the clothing and kit has been assembled, pack it into the panniers or saddlebags and weigh it. Then try and get the weight down. Ensure that the weight is evenly distributed and as low as possible, for this will help balance and steering. A trial run or two will concentrate minds most wonderfully on the weight and space problem. Please also note that panniers are not always necessary. The amount of kit that will go into a saddlebag is quite surprising.

**Gearing** At an early point in the planning stage, the cyclist should consider if the gearing on the bike is suitable for the terrain he or she intends to cover. In general most off-the-peg bikes are over-geared, but even when the normal adjustments have been made to reduce this inbuilt problem, the cyclist may still consider fitting a very low gear of under 30in, for touring the Alps, Pyrénées or the Vosges. If so, talk to the cycle shop and get this done during the pre-trip service (see pp 23–24).

**Tyres and tubes** For some curious and historic reason, the tyres and tubes commonly used on U.K. manufactured machines are not used on Continental cycles, and therefore not always available on the Continent. With the growing use of metrication, this problem is declining, but it is still a point to consider; 27in × 1.25in tyres and tubes are almost impossible to obtain on the Continent, and many tourists use the 26in × 1.25in tyre as it is a standard size abroad. The most common Continental size is the 700c, but if your particular cycle has 27in × 1.25in tyres, then you must carry a spare tyre and tubes with you.

**Service and spares** Before leaving on a major tour, the cycle must be thoroughly checked and serviced. If the tourist has the skill, this task need take no more than a Sunday morning, but check all the moving parts, adjust the brakes and gears, lubricate hubs and chain, making sure, or as sure as possible, that the machine is ready for hundreds of miles of touring. Things may still go 'twang', however, and since parts for British bikes may not be readily available in France, the cyclist should

take a few spare parts, in addition to some of the tools already
mentioned in Chapter 1. These spares might include:
1. A spare 1.5in cover (if applicable)
2. Two spare tubes
3. Rear gear cable
4. Rear brake cable (can be cut down for front brake)
5. Spare spokes
6. Spare brake blocks.
Some U.K. cycle shops will make up a 'tour kit' for the cyclist,
and allow the unused items to be returned for credit after the
trip.

**Servicing in France** It is always best if the cyclist can carry
out all the necessary maintenance and even repairs, without
using a cycle shop for anything more than the supply of spare
parts; at the very least the cyclist must be able to repair or
maintain the machine enough to get to the nearest repair shop.
Remember that many French garages will repair and service
bikes, particularly if you have the spare parts. The address of
the nearest cycle shop can be found in the *Bottin*.

**Getting fit** Once all the kit has been assembled, the cyclist
should pack the panniers most carefully, fit them to the bike,
and go out for a few runs. Aim to cover the intended daily
distance at least once, before you leave for France, for even
those who ride their cycle daily to work will find a vast difference between that and a 80km (50-mile) haul on a loaded
machine across some sunny hills in France. These trial runs
will concentrate the mind and get the tourist fit or at least
fitter, before the holiday begins.

**Touring technique** Successful and enjoyable touring is, to a
large extent, an attitude of mind. It should be a relaxing
pastime and the first urge to resist is the desire to ride half the
planned distance in the first day. Start slowly, and let the
mileage build up over the duration of the trip. Stop after an
hour or so for a coffee, and walk about to stretch the legs. If it
is getting warm, change into lighter garments, and check that
the panniers are in place and all is well before moving off again.
Remember the total distance for that day, or the whole trip,
and conserve your energy. Drink plenty of water, apply
suncream and lip salve until your face is used to the sun and
wind.

French hills tend to be longer than British ones, so use the
gears fully and climb steadily rather than in wild bursts. On
long descents ease off the brakes wherever possible or alternate

On the road in France.

the use of front and back brakes to prevent the rims overheating. On a very long descent stop for a while to let them cool.

Check the machine over daily, wiping off that day's grime, and carry out any necessary maintenance as you go along. Brake and gear cables may need adjustment after a few days, so have time allocated for on-tour servicing.

**Daily stages** The tours which follow are based on *average* daily stages of 80km., which most experienced tourists agree will be perfectly adequate and cover the ground at a pleasant pace. That does not mean 80km every day. Start slowly, and extend the distance as you become fitter and the terrain permits. I usually settle for 40–50km for the first couple of days, and find I am up to 100–120km per day by the end of a week, if the terrain is reasonable.

Wherever you go, take your time . . . you are travelling by cycle, so travel quietly, gently, rolling along, taking in the sights, soaking up the sun, relaxing, letting the pressure ease off. There is no better way to travel, no finer place to go, so with all our preparations made, let us put it all together and go cycletouring in France.

'One great fault of the English is their desire to discuss, over and over again, in the most tiresome manner, the next day's route.'

**T. J. Hogg,** *Two hundred and Nine Days*

# TOUR 1
# The Road to Agincourt
## 'Can this cockpit hold the vasty fields of France?' *Shakespeare,* Henry V

| | |
|---|---|
| Distance: | 480km (300 miles). |
| Provinces: | Normandy, Picardy, Pas de Calais-Nord. |
| Maps: | IGN Carte Touristique Rouge Nos. 102 (Normandie) and 101 (Pays du Nord, Picardie). |
| Guidebooks: | Christopher Hibbert, *Agincourt*, (Batsford). Lt. Col. A. H. Burne, *The Agincourt War*, (Eyre & Spottiswoode). |
| Ports: (out) | Night ferry, Southampton–Le Havre. |
| (home) | Calais or Boulogne to Dover or Folkestone. |
| Time required: | Seven days. |

**INTRODUCTION** This is a thematic tour which follows the route taken in 1415 by the English King, Henry V, from Harfleur to his victory at Agincourt. Thanks to a wealth of contemporary accounts, it is possible to trace this route with considerable accuracy, and it provides a good theme for a pleasant ride across some gentle countryside. The terrain, while pleasantly varied, is never demanding, the route takes in some interesting towns, and the region is well supplied with campsites and small *Logis*, hotels.

The Battle of Agincourt took place in October and when I rode the route, also in October, the weather was inclined to be dreary, so the spring or summer months might be more suitable, but at any time of the year this tour will provide the perfect introduction to cycletouring in France, for the average touring cyclist, the family group, and all lovers of history.

\* \* \*

The Road begins at the little town of Harfleur, now absorbed into the suburbs of the great French port of Le Havre. There is not much left of Shakespeare's 'girded Harfleur', except for some tumbled remnants of the curtain walls, and in the main square, a statue of the French knight who wrested the town back from the English at the end of the Hundred Years War.

Henry's siege of Harfleur was not a great success. He captured the town but lost a great many men in the process, mostly through sickness, and one small town was not much to show for all that effort. His decision to march overland to winter quarters at Calais, then an English possession, was therefore a political gesture, designed to demonstrate that he had the power to march anywhere he wished. On 7 October 1415 he left Harfleur and set out for the north, leading a small army of about 6000 men.

The first part of the Road leads up to Montivilliers (6.5km). From here the actual route is obscure, so follow the D925 for a short distance, and then bear left, along the D32, for Étretat,

The cliffs at Étretat

on the coast (28km). Before riding down to this little seaside resort, take the D111 and ride up to the top of the cliffs near Cap d'Antifer, for views down to the great cliff formations, hollowed out in the chalk by wave action.

Étretat is a pleasant little town with a sand and pebble beach, but after a coffee here, ride up and take the D11 coast road, past Yport to Fécamp (17km).

The chronicles say that Henry's army set fire to the town and ravished the female population, which seems unlikely. Fécamp today is a fishing port, and just the place for lunch. It is also famous for the abbey church of the Holy Trinity, which contains the Sanctuary of the Holy Blood, to which pilgrimages take place every year on the Tuesday and Thursday after Trinity Sunday. The town is perhaps even better known for the production of the liqueur called Benedictine after the monks who invented it hereabouts. The Benedictine distillery can be visited.

A stop at Fécamp might well complete the first day's run, but those who wish to continue have a choice of following the coast road (D79) with frequent steep descents into the valleys, or travelling inland to Cany-Barville (20km), on the D925. The coast road offers spectacular views across the Channel, and leads to St Valery-en-Caux, which has a youth hostel. This, incidentally, is the *pays de Caux*, the chalk country.

The next day's run leads across country, on the D70, to Offranville, and down to the great ruined castle at Arques-la-Bataille (40km). This castle was there when Henry's army filed beneath the walls, and the castle guns fired on them, but the battle that gives the place its name was fought more than a century later, in 1589, by Henry of Navarre against the forces of the Catholic League. There is a good small hotel, Au Vert Galant, just by the walls, and ideal for lunch, while the port of Dieppe is only 6km down the road.

After lunch, and a tour of the castle, the Road runs on, following the minor D454 to the borders of Normandy at Eu (31km) on the river Breste.

Eu is a pleasant town, with plenty of inexpensive accommodation. Try the Hotel Relais in the Place Albert 1er. The Château at Eu, which can be visited, was the favourite residence of Louis Phillipe, who twice entertained Queen Victoria here. The garden and park were laid out by Louis XIV's gardener, Le Nôtre.

By crossing the Bresle, we leave Normandy and follow Henry V's trail, up to the river Somme. Henry was following the route taken by his grandfather Edward III, who, before Crécy, crossed the Somme by the ford at Blanchetaque.

The route, still on minor roads, follows the D63 to Vaudricourt and then the D106 to the church at Boismont. The ford of Blanchetaque has long since vanished, but it probably lay between Boismont and a point across the river Somme between Noyelles and Port-le-Grand. There is a bridge now, but when Henry arrived there he found the causeways broken, the ford blocked by stakes and a large French army on the far bank. Unable to cross, he turned away from his route to safety and marched upstream, seeking another crossing place, while the French followed along the north bank, leading him deeper into France. Before leaving the mouth of the Somme, modern travellers should try to ride round to Le Crotoy, (17km), and have a meal at Chez Mado. The great dish of Picardy is the *ficelle picard*, a kind of pancake with onions and cheese – delicious!

The Road, now very flat and fast, follows the river up to Abbeville (15km), and then, still by the river, to Hangest-sur-Somme (26km), and Picquigny. From here the city of Amiens, capital of Picardy, is only a few miles away, and the Gothic cathedral there is well worth a visit. The tourist can take in a visit to this fine city before picking up Henry's trail again at Boves.

There is the remnant of another castle near Boves, but here the English army found a quantity of wine and, to Henry's considerable annoyance, got stupendously drunk. Order was restored when a soldier was hanged for stealing a pyx from the church at Boves, and duly chastened, the march continued.

As a glance at the map will reveal, above Amiens the Somme makes a great wide sweep, up to Peronne, and this gave Henry a chance to elude his pursuers. Leaving the river at Corbie he struck off south, across the neck of land, and following the D337, we can trace his route across the downland, through Chaulnes and Nesle and then up to the river again at Voyennes or Bethancourt (30km). Here Henry finally managed to cross the river, but as his army reached the far bank on the evening of 19th October, the main French army entered Peronne.

Our route crosses the Somme at Bethancourt, and on the far bank arrives at the village of Y . . . that's all, just Y, which is said to have the shortest placename in France.

The next stop is Peronne (19km), which has another fortress, and from Peronne we turn west across another and much bloodier battlefield, for this country is the old war-torn territory of the 1916 Battle of the Somme, which began on 1 July and lasted until the end of November, by which time over a million men had died. On 1 July, the British Army had 60,000 casualties before breakfast. Those who have gained a little time coming up the Somme could take half-a-day to ride around the Somme Battlefield, which lies astride the road which runs from Albert to Baupaume. Visit Thiepval, Fricourt, Delville Wood, and the Memorial Park at Auchonvilliers, where the Newfoundland Regiment lost 710 out of 900 men in 30 minutes and put their island into mourning. Above all this the Golden Virgin still stands over the church in Albert. During the Great War a shell struck the base of this statue and knocked it out, so that the Virgin hung out above the columns of soldiers marching up to the front. It was said to be lucky to march under the Golden Virgin of Albert, and that when she fell the war would end . . . as it did, three weeks after she fell, in 1918.

Meanwhile, back in 1415, Henry's damp little army plodded on across the downlands, trying to escape the French to safety, through Albert (24km), and then on today's D938 to Forceville (7km) and Acheux, and up to Lucheux (20km), on the minor roads to Pas-de-Artois. From here the army pressed on to Frévent, on the river Couche, and then following what is now the D104, veered north-west, for Blangy (35km) on the river Ternoise.

Here, on the 24 October 1415, an English scout crossed the river, and rode up to the far crest. What he saw appalled him, for the French army had managed to get in front and were now spilling across the plain ahead, blocking the road to Calais. He rode back to the King, crying, 'Arm quickly, for we are to fight a world of innumerable people.'

Henry and his captains rode out to view the French host and as night fell he moved his own army down into the village of Maisoncelles. The French filled the plain ahead, taking up all the land between the other villages. The one on the right was called Tramecourt and the one on the left, crowned by a small castle, was Agincourt. It was the eve of the 25 October, the feast of the Saints Crispin and Crispian.

\* \* \*

Accommodation is a trifle scanty in these small villages, so stay the night in St-Pol (16km from Agincourt) or Hesdin (18km) or at the one-star *Hotel D'Amiens*, a Logis de France at Frévent (23km). If the weather is reasonable, the surrounding farmers will usually permit camping. The final day can be spent exploring the battlefield and riding up to the coast at Calais or Boulogne for the ferry back to Britain.

The Syndicat d'Initiative of what is now called Azincourt, has erected signboards around the sites, illustrating the events of 1415, and there are a number of memorials. The Battle-line followed the line of the present small road which runs between Azincourt and Tramecourt, and the landscape has changed very little. The castle of Azincourt has gone, but the *motte* on which it stood can be seen in the farmyard at the centre of the village. The grave-pits, marked by a cross, lie to the left of the road to Ruisseauville, and the events are easy to follow.

The Battle lasted a little over two hours, and when it was over, 10,000 French lay dead. The English lost less than 200. According to the French historian, René de Belleville, *'jamais désastre aussi grande n'avait été infligé a la France,'* . . . but it gained the Plantagenet kings very little. Henry died, his conquests incomplete, in 1422, and seven years later Joan of Arc arrived and commenced the movement which was, by 1453, to move the English finally from France, where we go today as tourists, and as friends.

From Agincourt, follow minor roads north and west to Boulogne or Calais, a distance of around 50km or 70km (Calais) and, now that the cyclist is fit, a pleasant run with which to round off a visit to this historic part of France.

At last – Agincourt

# TOUR 2
# The Normandy Coast and D-Day Beaches

## 'A nation which forgets its history is doomed to relive it.'
### *G. Santayana*, Life of Reason

---

Distance:     450km (280 miles).

Province:     Normandy (Manche, Calvados, Seine-Maritime).

Maps:     IGN Carte Touristique Rouge No. 102. Michelin 1:200,000 No. 54 or Regional 1:200,000 no. 231.

Guidebooks:     David Howarth, *Dawn of D-Day*, (Collins). Cornelius Ryan, *The Longest Day*, (Collins). Chester Willmot, *The Struggle for Europe*, (Collins).

Ports: (out)     To Le Havre or Cherbourg.

    (home)     To Southampton or Portsmouth.

Time required:     Eight days.

**INTRODUCTION** This cycle ride, along the northern coastline of Normandy, offers those elements that any traveller will look for in France. On this road you will find splendid scenery, much history and great variety in architecture and terrain. For various reasons I have chosen to describe this tour from the west, starting in Cherbourg. It so happens that the D-Day Landings of 1944 (which the French, incidentally, call *J-Jour*) began in the Cotentin Peninsula on Utah Beach at 6.30 a.m. on 6th June. The Allied armies came ashore with the tide which turned up to one hour later, by the time the 3rd British Division came ashore on Sword Beach 50 miles to the east.

That fact apart, the Cotentin Peninsula is more attractive as an introduction to this province than the docks and refineries of Le Havre, so, for reasons of history, beauty and utility, I opted for Cherbourg and suggest you do the same.

**A BRIEF HISTORY OF D-DAY** Operation Overlord, the Allied invasion of German-occupied Europe, was the largest

amphibious landing in history. The Allies, under U.S. General Eisenhower and commanded in the field by the British General Montgomery, were attempting to establish a bridgehead on five beaches codenamed Utah, Omaha, Gold, Juno and Sword. They deployed on the first day, two American parachute divisions, the 88th and 101st, who landed in the Cotentin on the night of 5–6 June, the U.S. 4th Division who landed on Utah Beach, the U.S. 1st Division which was badly cut up on Omaha Beach, and further east, three British and Canadian Divisions, the 50th (Northumberland), the 3rd (Canadian) and the 3rd (British), who landed on Gold, Juno and Sword. The British 6th Airborne Division landed astride the Caen Canal. In addition there were U.S. Rangers, Commandos, tanks and artillery formations, carried in 3000 ships and supported by hundreds of aircraft. This force was opposed initially by four German divisions under Field Marshal Erwin Rommel. By the evening of D-Day the Allies were ashore on a 80km (50-mile) front, and Bayeux had been captured. Over 2500 men had been killed and total casualties on the first day exceeded 10,000. Nine months later, on 8 May 1945, the war in Europe ended.

The story of Operation Overlord is a fascinating tale and the cycletourist should read one of the background titles listed above in order to appreciate fully the events which took place on one dramatic day in this now peaceful province. It was not always as we see it today and the events that happened here should be remembered.

The terrain is fairly gentle and although this tour includes numerous diversions, a full week should be sufficient, with, say, a Friday night out and a Saturday night home, allowing eight clear days to cover the ground and see the sights at leisure. There are plenty of small hotels and campsites with youth hostels in Bayeux and Isigny-sur-Mer. Normal touring gears are sufficient.

Arriving early in Cherbourg, the cyclist can begin with a small diversion and ride west out of the town on the D45 towards the Nez de Joborg, This road is a scenic route with fine views over the Channel, and it is really too good to miss, giving a little taste of another ride south and west into Brittany. Follow the D45 at least as far as the viewpoint of the Roch du Castel Vendon, (12km) before returning through Cherbourg, which has a military museum in the Fort du Roule and, again taking the coastal road, head east on the D116 for Barfleur (35km). Barfleur is a delightful little fishing village and the food at the Phare is excellent.

From here, keep to the coast as far as St Vaast-la-Hougue and Quettehou, both sailing centres, and then go south to Ravenoville-Plage. Just south of here Utah Beach begins, but to keep the events in order turn east on the D15 for Ste-Mère-Église.

Ste-Mère-Église has a famous horse market, but we must see the Parachute Museum, under the parachute-style roof. This records the feats of the airborne forces of 1944, who actually landed in the square of Ste-Mère-Église, while the townspeople and Germans were fighting a fire. The church was used by snipers and the tower is still pock-marked with bullet holes. See the memorial window in the church and the museum before returning to Utah Beach. The U.S. 4th Infantry came ashore virtually unopposed at Utah, and joined up with the airborne forces over the next few days. There is a monument at La Madelaine. From here follow the D913 to St-Côme-du-Mont and Carentan, which has another museum, campsites and my favourite restaurant hereabouts, the Auberge Normande. This is flat, open, marshy country, and the route runs across the head of the bay to Isigny, where the butter comes from, and then left, on the D514 to Grandcamp and the cliff of the Pointe du Hoc (25km).

American Rangers scaled the Pointe du Hoc in broad daylight to knock out the coastal batteries, and from here the traveller gets a good view east to the coastline past Vierville. Here lies Omaha, bloody Omaha, where the U.S. 1st Infantry Division was cut to pieces. The Germans were well alert when the Big Red One came ashore, and their defenses could not be penetrated. The 1st Infantry lost 3000 men, killed and wounded in a long day's fighting where, as was said at the time, the only men on the beach were the dead and those who were going to die. It took warships engaging the enemy guns over open sights and a great deal of courage to move the 1st Infantry inland, but in the end they did it. It all looks very different today, but if you go to St. Laurent you will find the U.S. Military Cemetery, where many of that Division still hold the shore.

The road leads on over low cliffs to Port-en-Bessin, and here the traveller should turn inland for 9km to the old town of Bayeux. Most Normandy towns were badly damaged in the fighting after D-Day, but Bayeux was captured on the evening of 6 June without much street fighting and was therefore spared. It contains many fine old houses, a Battle of Normandy Museum, a cathedral and that marvellous relic of an earlier invasion, the Tapisserie de la Reine Mathilde, better known as the Bayeux Tapestry, which is actually an embroidery, ordered as a wall-hanging for Bayeux Cathedral by William the Conqueror's half-brother, Bishop Odo. Allow at least half a day for exploring Bayeux.

Next day take the D516 North to Arromanches-les-Bains (10km). Here is the D-Day Museum, a marvellous place to learn about the landings, with films, dioramas, models and displays of weaponry and equipment. Offshore in the bay, lie the caissons of the Mulberry Harbours, artificial harbours which the Allied Navy towed across the Channel to serve as a port until one could be captured and brought into service.

West of Arromanches lies Gold and then Juno. In Courselles (12km) a Sherman tank occupies pride of place in the square. This is a D-D (Duplex Drive) swimming tank, dredged from the sea years after D-Day. Beyond Courselles lie a string of little resort towns behind the wide sandy beaches, Luc-sur-Mer, St. Aubin and Langrune (31km). The beach here is vast for the tide goes out for over 2km.

Riva Bella (11km) is a suburb of Ouistreham, which stands at the seaward end of the Caen Canal. Turn inland here and ride up to Bénouville and Pegasus Bridge, captured by glider-borne troops of 6th Airborne just after midnight on the night of 5–6 June. Across the river around Ranville, lies the main 6th Airborne drop-zone, and the casements of the Merville Battery, captured by 9 Para after heavy fighting.

The Bayeux Tapestry

Caen, 11km from the sea, is the capital of Lower Normandy, and a very fine city indeed. Aim to spend at least one night in Caen and take time to explore the two abbeys, the Abbaye aux Hommes, where the Conqueror lies buried, and the Abbaye aux Dames, built by his wife, Mathilde. Caen Castle once held the Norman Court, and the town also contains a university, founded in the fifteenth century by John of Bedford, brother of Henry V.

Once past Caen we leave the D-Day battlefields behind us and ride across country on D-roads to Cabourg and Houlgate, two Edwardian-style resort towns on the coast. Of the two I prefer Houlgate. The countryside inland is rather more hilly, so stay on the coast for fashionable Deauville and Trouville (20km). These are very crowded in the summer, and very French. From Deauville the traveller has a choice; to turn inland for 12km to Pont l'Evêque or press on north and east to Honfleur . . . or both. If in doubt choose Honfleur, a port, a yachting centre, a place for artists and painters, desperately picturesque. There are fine views across to the smokey towers of Le Havre from the hills behind Honfleur, and this again is a place to spend time in.

From Honfleur the D580 and various minor roads lead to the valley of the Risle and Pont Audemer (25km). Turn north here into the Parc Naturel Regional de Brotonne, a well-wooded region, straddling the Seine. Travel across this part of Normandy through Bourneville and Hauville to cross the Seine by

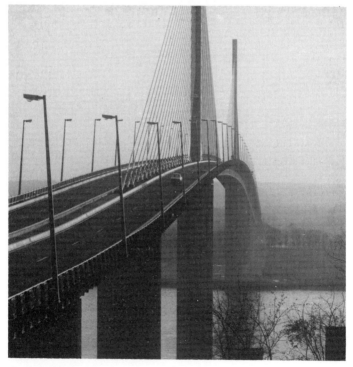

Pont de Brotonne

ferry (*bac*) at Port Jumièges. The ferry crossing takes only a few minutes and cycles travel free. Once across it is a short ride to the splendid ruins of the Abbaye of Jumièges and then up this neck of land to the D982 and the riverside town of Caudebec-en-Caux under the web-like cabling of the Pont de Brotonne. If you are lucky, ocean-going ships will be gliding past up the river, for Rouen, although many miles from the sea, is a great port.

From Caudebec the ferry port at Le Havre is only 50km away, but the river road, though fast, can be crowded with heavy *camions*. If time permits, take the D982 to Lillebonne and then one of the minor roads south and west towards Harfleur and home.

*  *  *

This ride will introduce the cycletourist to a part of France which has many links with the U.K. It may even feel quite like home, and much of Normandy does indeed resemble part of Sussex and Hampshire. The food is rich and excellent, the cider strong, and the Calvados brandy memorable. So if you like Normandy, why not visit the province again and explore the other *départements* of the Eure and the Orne. It's a big province and there is still much more to see.

# TOUR 3
# A Tour of Normandy
## 'The world belongs to him that has seen it.' *Lord Avebury*

| | |
|---|---|
| Distance: | 973km (600 miles). |
| Province: | Normandy (Manche, Orne, Calvados, Eure, Seine-Maritime). |
| Maps: | IGN Carte Rouge Normandy no. 102. Michelin 1:200,000 Regional no. 231. |
| Guidebooks: | Nesta Roberts, *Companion Guide to Normandy*, (Collins). |
| | Michelin Green Guide, *Normandy*. |
| Ports: (out) | To Cherbourg or Dieppe. |
| (home) | To Newhaven, Southampton, Portsmouth. |
| Time required: | Two weeks or 12 days. |

**INTRODUCTION** This tour, as described below, will take the traveller in a wide sweep through every *département* of the province of Normandy, visiting every major place of interest. The terrain is varied, often hilly but never mountainous, so normal touring gears will be quite adequate. Care has been taken to minimise the overlap between this tour and the two previous ones, while including all the major places, such as Caen and Bayeux, which cannot be overlooked in any tour of this historic province. Even so, to keep the mileage reasonable, a number of places have had to be left out and as usual the traveller is urged to wander, cutting corners here and there. This route is not a tightrope, and you can leave it without any fear of missing much of importance, for there is plenty to see, although this tour is designed to visit some less well-known places, or reach popular ones by minor roads. To save time I recommend the night boats to Dieppe or Cherbourg, and home again, so that a full day can be spent on the road if necessary. If the trip overruns and time gets short, there are trains from Rouen to Dieppe and from major towns in the Cotentin to Cherbourg. I have, as before, chosen to cover the route from Cherbourg, and begin with a tour down the Cotentin.

\* \* \*

From Cherbourg turn west and head out on the D45 along the coast road to Audeville and then round the Baie Ecalgrain to the Nez de Jobourg (45km). Those who know Normandy well claim, with some reason, that this is the most picturesque part of the entire province. Visit the little port of Goury and enjoy the views across to the Channel Islands.

The 'D' roads south along this western edge of the province are nearly all fringed green on the maps, the sign of a picturesque route. Visit Biville (13km) and take the D117 road for Carteret (36km), avoiding the D904, which carries a lot of tourist traffic in the summer. From Carteret boats sail to Jersey and there is a good beach. Portbail is one of those little-known places, well worth a visit.

From here many small roads run south to Coutainville (50km) but the D650 is a good one, and from here a scenic route leads round the Sienne estuary, towards Coutances (13km). From Montmartin the D20 and D135 lead to Granville, which has a fine port and ramparts by Vauban. The coast road, through Carolles, leads over the clifftops to Avranches (33km). Here the traveller has a choice, but must turn west and visit Mont-St-Michel, the great fortress-abbey on a rock, standing out in the bay. Allow half a day to ride out and see it from Avranches on the D288 (22km).

From Avranches, ride east to Mortain (40km) on the D911 through Brécey. Mortain is a little hilltop town on the edge of the Parc Normandie-Maine, which straddles the southern frontier between the Orne department and the Sarthe, and a short ride on the D907 leads into the park, and to Domfront (25km), another hilltop town, and it's a stiff climb up there from the valley of the Varenne. Follow the D908 to Bagnoles de L'Orne (22km), a spa town, with lakes and many hotels, in the middle of the woods, where our route turns north, for the Roche d'Oëtre, the Orne gorges, and the hilly country called the Suisse Normande. Take the D20 and the D21 through Briouze, to La Fôret Auvray. If time permits, a day off here might be a good idea, for the countryside is very beautiful and the hills are steep. Then move on to Falaise (22km) to see the great castle where the Conqueror was born, well worth half a day of your time.

After Falaise, the route turns north and west across the Suisse Normande, a tough ride but after several days in the saddle the rider should be fit. Head for Clécy, then down the Orne on the D562, turning west for Aunay-sur-Orne, and up on the D22 (in the direction of Caen) to Bayeux. This is a long ride of 112km (70 miles) but if the Suisse Normande can be tackled early in the day, the traveller should arrive in Bayeux by nightfall. Bayeux and Caen, 27km to the east, are, with Falaise, the historic heart of Normandy. The two are worth at least a day each to see the Bayeux Tapestry, the Castle of the Conqueror, and the two abbeys, in Caen.

Falaise Castle

You could spend a gentle day, spread between Bayeux and Caen, and then head out, south-east to St-Pierre-sur-Dives (32km), then the D102 and D35 to Trun, Chambois and the Haras du Pin, the French National Stud, which is well worth visiting to see the horses and foals. This is the Perche country, famous for horsebreeding, (44km).

From the Haras, the traveller heads for the Seine, across country, through Exmes, St Evroult and then on the D37 and D830 to Conches (80km). Overnight here, then take the D61 to Acquigny (40km). From Acquigny it is a scant 25km to the riverside town of Les Andelys, and the ruins of Richard Lionheart's great fortress, the Château Galliard.

The Seine bends and swoops across this part of Normandy, so follow the river part of the time, climbing the high ground across the neck of land to the Côte des Deux Amants. Here, so it is said, a peasant lad was promised the hand of a nobleman's daughter if he could run up the hill with her in his arms. He succeeded but dropped dead at the top; be glad you have gears. And so to Rouen.

Rouen is a major port and a big city with lots to see and do. It will take even the devoted tourist at least a day to see the old quarter, the Gros Horloge, the Old Market, where Joan of

Arc was burned, the churches, and the fine houses. This is another city, like Caen and Bayeux, where it pays to stroll around.

From Rouen to Dieppe is only 60km, a pleasant run north through Cléres, Auffay, and so at last over the hill past the water tower painted by the artist Varesely, and down to the ferry port.

# TOUR 4
# Eastern Brittany

**'In the East, my pleasure lies.'**
***Shakespeare,*** *Antony and Cleopatra*

---

| | |
|---|---|
| Distance: | 630km (390 miles). |
| Province: | Brittany (Côtes-du-Nord, Ille-et-Vilaine, Morbihan). |
| Maps: | IGN Carte Touristique No. 5 Bretagne. Michelin 1:200,000 Nos. 59 and 63, or Regional No. 230. |
| Guidebooks: | Michelin Green Guide, *Brittany*. |
| | Neil Lands, *History, People and Places in Brittany*, (Spurbooks). |
| | Keith Spence, *Brittany and the Bretons, (Gollancz)*. |
| | Henry Myhill, *Brittany*, (Faber). |
| Ports: (out) | To St-Malo. |
| (home) | To Portsmouth. |
| Time required | Two weeks or 10 days. |

**INTRODUCTION** This tour through the eastern *départements* of Brittany begins with a ten-hour voyage from the U.K. through the Channel Islands to the Breton port of St-Malo. The terrain of eastern Brittany is relatively gentle and the weather usually mild; both may be compared to that which the cyclist might expect to find in Cornwall, with which Brittany and the Bretons have close historic and cultural links. Normal U.K. gearing will be sufficient, there are plenty of campsites, gîtes d'étape, and small hotels. The food is excellent and plentiful, especially if you like seafood, while for a mid-day snack try a crêpe—the Breton pancake made of buckwheat flour—and a glass of cider.

This tour takes in some of the finest tourist sights in France as well as many of those little-known places where the (other) tourists don't go. There is much to see, notably such places as St-Malo, Mont-St-Michel, Vitré, Dinan and Rennes, and the distances are small enough to allow time for visits.

\* \* \*

Our tour begins on the night-time Brittany Ferry from Portsmouth to St-Malo. This ancient fortress town, a refuge for corsairs during the Napoleonic Wars, is well worth exploring. There is a good walk round the ramparts, and if the tide is out you can walk across to the Grande Bé, a small island where the writer René de Châteaubriand is buried. See the corsair city, destroyed in 1944, but now restored, which is called the Inter-Muros. The history of St-Malo is displayed in the Town Museum in the Town Hall.

From St-Malo ride east to the suburb of Paramé (5km), and then take the coast-road, past Rotheneuf and then the D201 to the Pointe-du-Grouin and then to Cancale (22km). Cancale is a pretty port and a great place for lunch in one of the restaurants on the quai. From here there is a view on a clear day to Mont-St-Michel, 40km away across the bay.

Stick to the coast road (D155) to Pontorson (48km). From here it is a short 9km to the abbey-fortress of Mont-St-Michel, a spectacular sight on the rock out in the bay. This is reached by a causeway, and a decent visit will take half a day to explore the town and abbey. Buy a scallop-shell pilgrim badge from the tourist office by the main gate. There is very little accommodation in Mont-St-Michel but Pontorson has both hotels and campsites.

From Pontorson, which actually lies just in Normandy, we go east for a while into Normandy on the D30 to St-James (14km), to see the U.S. military cemetery. Then take the D798 south for a few kilometres and then fork right on the D102 to Montours and the D17 to Fougères (22km). Fougères has a huge castle which once defended Brittany's frontier against the French—that lot from Paris and points east! There is a good view of the castle from the public gardens.

From Fougères take the D178 south for a while then fork left on the D108 to Parce, the Étang de Chatillon, and so to Vitré (28 km). This route follows minor roads and avoids the heavy traffic on the more direct D178. Vitré is another fortress city, a very formidable place, and a must for all those interested in the Middle Ages.

At Vitré our route turns west and south. I suggest a route which follows the D777 for 14km then left towards Bais, and the D110 for Rétiers and the Roche aux Fées, 15km. From here the route lies west to the Château of Le Plessis, Bain-de-Bretagne, then the D53 for St-Just, Gacilly and Rochefort-en-Terre. There are a host of minor roads on this route, but the total distance from Rétiers is around 100km.

North of Rochefort-en-Terre, which is a pleasant yet little-known town, lie the moors of the Landes de Lanvaux, which resemble Exmoor. Follow the road directly north to Malestroit

(16km) and then the D764 and D4 to Josselin (30km). Josselin has the great castle of the Dukes of Rohan, one of the great Breton families, and it is well worth a visit.

Twelve kilometres east of Josselin lies the town of Ploërmel, but stop about half way at the obelisk which marks the site of the Battle of the Thirty, which took place here in the year 1351. This Battle, a kind of murderous tournament between the

Dinan, the Clock Tower

English Knights of Ploërmel and the French garrison of Josselin, resulted in victory for the French, eight Englishmen being killed and the rest captured.

From Ploërmel take the minor road D141 north-east for the Val-Sans-Retour and the Forest of Paimport (15km). This is, according to legend, Arthurian country, the home of Sir Lancelot du Lac and Morgan-le-Fay. The curious object hereabouts is the so-called Stone of Merlin (*perron de Merlin*) in which Morgan imprisoned Arthur's wizard. To find this after the Val-Sans-Retour, find Folle Pensée, and at the far end of the village follow signs for the Fontaine de Baranton. With luck you will eventually find it, a spring in the woods, and legend has it that if you sprinkle the stone with water it will rain; the locals try it every time there is a drought.

There are several roads across the Fôret de Paimpont, but the D71-D30 to Montfort (25km) and then the D125 to Rennes, the present capital of the province, offer a good route. Rennes is a big place, a university city, with plenty to see and do. If time is pressing it will be possible to take the train from here back to St-Malo. If time still permits though, go due north on the D82, to Combourg, Châteaubriand's home (38km). Here turn west, risking a major road for once, the D794 for 24km, to Dinan, a perfect gem of a medieval town and the ideal place as the final, most memorable part of any trip. Dinan was the birthplace of Bertrand du Guesclin who, as Constable of France, led the French armies against the English forces of the Black Prince, during the Hundred Years War. His statue stands in the main square, and his heart is buried in the Church of St-Sauveur. Spend half a day in Dinan, ride down to the Rance, and then take the minor road, D12, along the Rance to the big tidal barrage and then up past the 15th century Tour Solidor, back to the Inter-Muros of St-Malo, and the ferry home. You will have seen some splendid sights, great castles, wild country, and gained a taste for Brittany that is sure to bring you back.

# TOUR 5
# Western Brittany
## 'And beyond that, the Atlantic wide!'
### *Matthew Arnold*

| | |
|---|---|
| Distances: | Two-week itinerary—800 km (500 miles). |
| | Three-week itinerary—1045 km (660 miles). |
| Province: | Brittany (Finistère and Morbihan). |
| Maps: | IGN Carte Touristique No. 5. Michelin |
| | Regional 1:200,000 No. 230 or Nos. 58, 59, 63. |
| Guidebooks: | Michelin Green Guide, *Brittany*. |
| | Keith Spence, *Brittany and the Bretons*, (Gollancz). |
| | Neil Lands, *A Visitor's Guide to Brittany*, (Moorland). |
| | Henry Meyhill, *Brittany*, (Faber). |
| Port: (out) | To Roscoff. |
| (home) | To Plymouth. |
| Time Required: | Two or three weeks. |

**INTRODUCTION** By history and tradition Brittany is divided into two distinct regions. In Celtic times, before the Romans came, what is now Brittany was called *Armorica*, 'the land facing the sea,' and the province today has over 1000km of coastline. The inland parts were known as the *Argoat*, the 'country of wood', although Brittany today is not particularly well wooded. These two, Argoat and Armorica, are our first divisions.

The second divide lies between the eastern provinces which have been influenced by France proper—for Brittany is a province apart—and the very Breton *départements* to the west, the ground we shall cover on this ride. Here we will find the *calvaries*, the curious, heavily carved parish-enclos of the 16th century, the ladies in their traditional coiffes, and if we are lucky, even hear the Breton language. The winds, if they blow, will blow from the west, and it can be showery even in summer, so don't forget the rain gear. As the birdlife is prolific round the coastline which makes up the bulk of the journey, a fieldguide and binoculars might add a great deal to the pleasures of the holiday. The terrain is moderate and no special gearing is required.

\* \* \*

Our trip begins with a night passage from Plymouth to Roscoff, from where we head directly south on the D769 to the Château de Penhoat. From here a minor road leads down to the D18 and at St-Thégonnec, 25km, the first of our parish-enclos. These large, beautifully carved calvaries were built in the sixteenth century during the Counter-Reformation as symbols of civic pride and apart from the calvary, the enclos consists of the church itself, and an ossuary—or boneyard. They are unique to Brittany, well worth seeing, and the one at St-Thégonnec and the two others at nearby Guimiliau and Lampaul-Guimileau (12km) are arguably the finest in Brittany.

The Calvary of St Thégonnac (detail)

From Lampaul go north to Landivisiau, and then follow the D32 to le Folgoët (23km). The museum here is a Renaissance jewel and the walls are emblazoned with the arms of the Duchess Anne, the last ruler of an independent Brittany, but only give yourself a brief halt here, for west of le Folgoët lie the Abers, deep, fjord-like estuaries, which are very beautiful. Take the D32 for Plouguerneau, then the D13 and D28 across the Abers and so to Portsall on the coast (35km). From here a marvellous route, the D27, follows the road south, with views to the isle of Ouessant (Ushant), as far as Le Conquet (32km).

The coastline here is very beautiful, but better things lie further south, so it's up and away through the port and naval base at Brest and down to Daoulas (45km) and over the small coastal hills and down to Le Faou (20km).

West to Le Faou lies the peninsula or *presq'île* of Crozon. Head directly for Crozon (27km). From here, take a ride to the three points of the peninsula, to the Pointe des Espagnols, to Camaret, a beautiful port, and to Morgat, 45km. Allow a day for this because if the weather is fine you will be often stopping for a swim or to admire the view.

The Standing Stones of Carnac

From Crozon go south and east under the loom of the Menez-Hom, a high peak of Brittany at 330m, before arriving at Locronan, (45km). Locronan is a beautiful historic town, with cobbled streets, and must be visited. After that we go west again, to the fishing port of Douarnenez (14km) and across the peninsula to Audierne (22km). From Audierne ride west, out to the spectacular if tourist-infested headland at the Pointe du Raz. This overlooks the Raz de Sein (15km), a fearsome seascape when the gales are blowing. Back at Audierne follow the road to Plozévet (10km) and then the D2 all the way south-east to Pont-l'Abbé and the yachting centre at Bénodet, (32km). Follow the river Odet upstream on the D20, a very minor road, to Quimper (15km) which has a fine cathedral and a Breton museum.

**Three-week itinerary** Those with only two weeks to spare must turn north at Quimper, but those with three weeks can continue as follows.

From Quimper go out on the D783 for Concarneau (18km), a walled town and fishing port, and then to Pont Aven (14km), a pretty spot, popular with artists; 4km past Pont Aven take the D24 right to Guidel (20km). Avoid Lorient, a naval base and port, and instead make for Hennebont (26km). This means a detour up the valley of the Scorff, but that is no hardship and Hennebont is attractive, with a huge cathedral.

After Hennebont run down 11 km to two attractive places, Etel, and the little island of St-Cado, across the Devil's Bridge, and then pass on to the menhirs of Carnac (12km). No one really knows who built, or rather planted the great lines of standing stones at Carnac, but the site is impressive. From Carnac it's a pleasant ride out to the tip of the Quiberon peninsula, before turning north to Auray (13km) and commencing a run across the Argoat to the north coast. If time permits though, take one of the Vedette Verte boats, which ply on the Morbihan, the 'little sea' and visit the Ile des Moines (Monks' Island) and the walled city of Vannes. Allow a day for this worthwhile diversion.

From Auray strike north, on the minor D19 for Pluvigner (13km) and then up to Baud (12km) to see the curious statue of the Venus de Quinipily, which is probably Greek. Then take the D142 and follow the Valley of the Blavet up to Pontivy (30km). From Pontivy, a good fast D road, the D767 which carries us north through Mur-de-Bretagne, past the Lac de Guerledan and up to Guingamp (65km) with good views half way at la Clarté. Guingamp is said to be the place where weavers invented gingham, but carry on north to Tréguier (30km) in the centre of the Granit Rose coast, where the last part of the journey begins and we link with the two-week itinerary.

**Two-week itinerary—continued** From Quimper go north and take the D785 for Briec (17km). Turn right on the D72 and so up to Châteauneuf du Faou (20km) then the D36 and D14 for Huelgoat (26km) capital of the Argoat, in the Parc Regional d'Armorique. This lies below the long ridges of the Montagnes d'Arrée, but these are Breton mountains and the highest is only 384m (just over 1000ft) high. From Huelgoat take the D14 for Berrien (5km), then the D42 north under the motorway and up to Lannion (60km), a most attractive scenic route, which is usually spared heavy traffic. From Lannion travel 18km east to Tréguier, where the two itineraries combine for the last day or so.

A light ending to a tour is always pleasant, but no one should leave Western Brittany without a visit to the red rocks of the Granit-Rose coast around Tréguier. Try and allow two days for this, for a tour east from Tréguier to Paimpol, and north to Port Blanc, a lovely spot. Visit the cathedral in Tréguier, which holds the tomb of St-Yves, patron saint of lawyers, before setting off, as close to the sea as possible to Trégastel and Perros-Gurec, 25km, and so down to Lannion (12km). From Lannion take the D201 to St. Michel-en-Grève and follow the coast road round to Locquirec before dropping down through Lanmeur to Morlaix (40km). From Morlaix it is 28km north, through St-Pol-de-Léon to the ferry port at Roscoff.

*　*　*

Both itineraries demand that the cyclist keep at it and maintains a good though not excessive daily average if time is to be found for half days on the beach, and time off to go sightseeing. However, the corners can be cut here and there and either route displays some famous and not so famous parts of these attractive and historic departements of Brittany. My advice is to ride the main roads and linking sections as quickly as possible, and early in the day, leaving time to explore the parts that interest you in the afternoons or on days off.

ORLEANS

BOURGES

LA FERTE ST. AUBIN

MEHUN SUR
YEVRE

LA FERTE
IMBAULT

VIERZON

CHAMBORD

MILLANCAY

BRACIEUX

BLOIS

CHAUMONT

CHENONCEAUX

AMBOISE

TOURS

VILLANDRY

LANGEAIS

AZAY LE RIDEAU

LOIRE

CHINON

FONTEVRAUD

POITIERS

SAUMUR

GENNES
ST. GEORGES DES
SEPT VOIES

ANGERS

ROCHEFORT

N

CHALONNES

INGRANDES

MONTJEAN

ST. FLORENT

ANCENIS

LIRE

CHAMPTOCEAUX

0  10  20  30  40  50  60  70  80  90  100

NANTES

KILOMETRES

LOIRE

LA ROCHELLE

# TOUR 6
# Along the Loire

**'Heureux qui, comme Ulysse, a fait un beau voyage.'**     *Joachim du Bellay*

---

| | |
|---|---|
| Distances: | One-week itinerary—513km (320 miles) Nantes to Orleans. Two-week itinerary—644km (400 miles) Nantes to Bourges. |
| Provinces: | Val de Loire (Anjou, Touraine, Berri), Central France. |
| Maps: | IGN Carte Touristique Nos. 106 (Val de Loire), 108 (Nivernais-Burgogne). Michelin 1:200,000: Nos. 63, 64, 65, 69; or Regional 1:200,000. Nos. 232 and 238. |
| Guidebooks: | Michelin Green Guide, *Chatêaux of the Loire*, (English). |
| | R. Dutton, *Châteaux of France*, (Batsford). |
| | Richard Wade, *Companion Guide to the Loire*, (Collins). |
| Ports: (out) | To St-Malo, or via Channel ports and Paris. |
|      (home) | To Portsmouth or via Paris/Calais/Boulogne to Dover/Folkestone. |
| Time required: | One, or two weeks. |

**INTRODUCTION** The Loire is the longest river in France. It rises in the Gerbier de Jonc, in the Ardèche, and runs for over 600 miles before it reaches the Atlantic west of Nantes, and it passes through some highly varied country on the way. Our ride (or rides) as described below, covers the historic parts of the Loire, between Nantes and Bourges, first through the castle country of Anjou, then the château country of Touraine, and finally into Berri, the very heartland of France.

For lovers of France, this ride has the lot; good weather, splendid castles, historic buildings, good food, excellent wines—and level roads, mostly, for we follow the river, or rivers for most of the way, and valleys tend to be flat. I chose to ride upstream rather than follow the flow, mainly because the ports make it more convenient but also because the countryside improves as you ride inland.

There are diversions. Some of the so-called châteaux of the Loire are not on the Loire at all. They are either inland or on other rivers. Chenonceaux, for example, is on the Cher, and the great château-fort of Chinon is on the Vienne. I should explain here that any great country house can be a château, but the medieval fortress, with battlements, is a château-fort. On this journey we shall see plenty of both, and always there is the river, the great Loire. In summer the river is quiet, barely trickling between the sandbanks, but see it in spring or after the autumn rains, and the Loire becomes a mighty, powerful flow, sweeping all before it as it surges to the sea.

\* \* \*

As the Loire valley lies in central France and our tour begins at Nantes, we begin with a train journey from St-Malo to Nantes via Rennes. As the distances are not vast and the route fairly direct, it *should* be possible to carry the bike as hand luggage on a through-ticket loading and off-loading it yourself. By rail, St-Malo to Rennes is 81km, and Rennes to Nantes 162km. You should take the night boat which (out Friday, home Sunday) gives eight clear days in France for the shorter journey. If the cycle has to go ahead, send it on and devote a day to exploring St-Malo or Dinan.

Nantes, former capital of Brittany, is a great port and city. The castle of the Dukes of Brittany stands behind its moat, and contains several museums, while the town is a thriving commercial centre well worth at least half a day of your time.

Leave Nantes by the south bank, on the D751 for Champto-ceaux (32km). Not only is this route quieter and more attractive than the road on the north bank, but it also leads through the Muscadet country, the great wine of the western Loire. Try a chilled bottle with a grilled trout and you'll have the meal of a lifetime. At Champtoceaux ride to the viewpoint of the Prom-enade de Champalud, before pressing on and crossing the river for Ancenis (17km), which is nothing special but a great wine centre and the river here is still tidal, 80km from the sea.

Recross the bridge and pass through Liré (3km), and bear left for St-Florent (13km), on a high hill. Bear left after St-Florent onto the D210 and follow this to Ingrandes, a lovely spot best viewed from the river bridge; then still on the D210 to Montjean (14km) and on to Challones (9km). After Challones we have to climb a bit up to the Corniche Angevine for a good view across the river and a reminder that we are now in the territory of the mighty counts of Anjou, who had the Devil for their ancestor and the kings of England as descendants. In the twelfth century, Count Geoffrey married Matilda, daughter of Henry I, and their son, Henry II, and his descendants ruled England and most of

Europe from Scotland to the Pyrénées for much of the next 300 years. Count Geoffrey loved hawking and to improve the cover for game birds he had the curious habit of carrying gorse cuttings in his hat or helmet and planting them whenever he stopped. In Latin- or French-gorse is *'genista'* or 'genet', and it is as the 'Plant-a-genet' that he and his family are known to history.

Across the river lies the moated château of Serrant, but you will have your fill of châtaux on this journey, so ride past medieval Rochefort (19km) and across the river to the great city of Angers, capital of Anjou, (25km). This route now takes you across the river and to the foot of the great castle. This was not built by the counts but completed in 1240 by Louis VII, Saint Louis. It has a drawbridge and a dry moat, eighteen towers and a marvellous collection of tapestries. See the castle and the Cathedral of St-Maurice, which has the original stained glass, and for something different, the Hôpital de St-Jean, a medieval hospital founded by Henry II to atone for the murder of Thomas à Becket.

We must get on, so it is back across the river, then left on the D751, inland a little past St-Georges-des-Sept-Voies, and back, through the woods, down to the river at Gennes (26km). It's quite hilly hereabouts, but the hills do give good views and break up the ride, while back on the D751 again on to Saumur (15km) the road is gentle.

Saumur is a splendid place. Ride out onto the bridge for a view of the castle, a fourteenth century fortress built by Louis Duc d'Anjou. It contains a Musée du Cheval, a Museum of the Horse, which is appropriate because Anjou is a centre for the French Cavalry who ride in tanks today, but keep the memory green with that famous cavalry display team, the Cadre Noir, the Black Squadron, which is based in Saumur, Visit the Syndicat d'Initiative, 25 rue Beaurepaire, and find out if the Cadre Noir are giving a display and if they are, don't miss it. There is also a magnificent military tattoo at the end of July, which I managed to catch on my ride down to Sète, (see Tour 20). Allow half a day for Saumur and then leave on the D145 for Fontevraud (15km). Fontevraud is the Plantagenet mausoleum, and the early counts and kings were all buried here. The abbey still contains the coloured effigies of Richard Coeur de Lion, his mother Eleanor of Aquitaine, his father Henry II, and Isabel of Angoulême, the wife of King John Lackland. There are guided tours but the abbey is closed from 12 noon to 2 pm each day, and closes for the evening at 7p.m. After visiting the abbey, ride out towards the D117 and then down to Chinon (35km). Seen from the south bank of the Vienne, the castle of Chinon looks intact, but only a shell actually remains. Chinon is very historic, full of medieval houses, and well worth a visit. There is a good campsite by the bridge. It was here, in 1429, that Joan of Arc met her 'gentil Dauphin' and obtained command of an army with which she raised the siege of Orleans. Today the little town lives on tourism and the good local wine, and is certainly one place in the Loire valley the traveller must not miss.

To return to the Loire proper, take the D751 which travels

A typical medieval street in Chinon

through the woods to the beautiful Château of Azay-le-Rideau (21km). Azay is a Renaissance château-fort, built in the late sixteenth century on the site of a medieval castle. It contains the famous nude painting of Gabrielle d'Estrées, mistress of Henry IV. After Azay, to get a feast of châteaux, ride to Lure (16km) and down to the Loire again at Langeais (5km), which is a château-fort with turrets and drawbridge, the place where Anne of Brittany married Charles VIII in 1491, and full today of fifteenth and sixteenth-century furniture and hangings.

We *must* get on, so back across the river and so up the D7 to Villandry (20km), one of the classic Loire châteaux with splendid formal gardens, and so we arrive at the good city of Tours (12km), the capital of Touraine, the garden of France. Tours is fairly industrial but the heart of the old city, where Joan of Arc's armour was made, still exists, together with the cathedral and the old houses in the rue Colbert.

After Tours we veer south on the D82, along the river Cher to visit the most beautiful château in France, Chenonceaux (33km). Try and get there in the morning, when the sun is rising, for the view from the eastern side is the finest. The Château of Chenonceaux belonged to the beguiling Diane de Poitiers, mistress of Henry II. When he was killed in a joust, his wife Catherine de Medici forced Diane to exchange Chenonceaux for her own château of Chaumont. There is a problem with constant château visiting; the tours take time and the cost starts to mount. The fee for Chenonceaux last year was 12 francs, so one has to be selective, but Chenonceaux itself is a must. From Chenonceux, ignoring the medieval towers of Montrichard, we take the D31 and ride north through the woods and down to Amboise (15km). Amboise is a very old town and full of interesting sites. Visit the Église St-Denis and the great château where Charles VIII came to an untimely end, smashing his skull against a door lintel, and from where, in 1560, the lords and ladies of the court assembled at the windows to watch the soldiers of the Catholic League murdering their prisoners. 1200 men were hanged from trees and the pinnacles of the castle.

Crossing the river again, we follow the D751 to Chaumont (18km). Chaumont stands above the river and it's a long walk from the gate to the château. Be nice to the gatekeeper and he may let you ride. The most interesting feature of Chaumont is the room occupied by Queen Catherine's astrologer, full of strange signs. After Chaumont, cross the river to the north bank and take minor roads through the forest, to Blois (20km).

Blois is smaller than Tours or Orleans, but rather grander, a very old town and home of the counts of Blois, sometime rivals to the Plantagenets of Anjou. See the Cathedral of St-Louis and the château, where Henri, Duc de Guise, was murdered in 1589. I like Blois and if you are by now feeling like a day off, then I recommend Blois as the place to enjoy it.

Château Chaumont

North-east of Blois lies mighty Chambord (15km), standing in parkland, surrounded by a wall twenty miles long! They do a *son-et-lumière* at Chambord, and it's well worth seeing. François I built Chambord as a hunting lodge—some lodge—but it was still incomplete when he died in 1559. Chambord is the last of the Loire chateaux I visited on this tour, but there are plenty more if you have the time and liking for them: Chéverny, Beaugency, Loches—a grim pile—and several others. They were built as refuges from the plagues which swept Paris, and because the great forests were full of stags for hunting. South of Chambord it is all forest, many hundreds of square miles, almost to Bourges. See below for the route from Chambord to Bourges.

To make a pleasant end to this journey, take the D33 east from Chambord and ride to La Ferte St. Aubin, before turning north to end this tour of the Loire in the city of St Joan, Orleans (70km).

I strongly recommend taking a guidebook with you on this journey, because the detail of each place requires more space to describe them than I have here. I took Richard Wade's *Companion Guide to the Loire*, and found it informative and very readable.

Orleans is a rail junction and there is a railway line along the Loire which may come in handy if you run out of time. To get back, *either* return to Nantes (300km) for the train to St-Malo, *or* return via Paris (130km) and so to the Channel ports.

Château Chambord

Those on a two-week trip can and should make more time for sightseeing, because the extra distance to Bourges is not great. Chambord stands on the northern edge of one of the largest forests in France. Head south and east, first on the D112, and so across the forest, through Bracieux, Millancay, which is surrounded by scores of little lakes, La Ferte-Imbault, and so to Vierzon, (63km) on the Cher.

From here take the minor D60 east to Mehun-sur-Yèvre (15km) and on to Bourges, one of the great cities of Central France, dominated by a really massive cathedral, a splendid end to this tour of splendours.

From Bourges there are direct trains to Paris and so home via the Channel ports.

\* \* \*

This tour can be accomplished to Orleans in one week or Bourges in two. In practice, the limiting factors are not the distance or terrain, but the traffic and the sightseeing. My tour went on to Bourges, because after a week on the road I was suffering from château-glut. I recommend taking two weeks and limiting the châteaux to two a day, but taking in at least one *son-et-lumière* performance, preferably the one at Chenonceaux which is the finest.

Another problem, certainly in summer, is the traffic, cars and touring coaches particularly. Use minor roads and narrow short cuts to avoid the worst of this almost unavoidable problem.

SAARBRUCKEN

BITCHE

KOHLHUTTE          LICHTENBERG
WINGEN             WIMMENAU
                   INGWILLER
LA PETITE PIERRE   WEITERSWILLER
                   NEUWILLER
PHALSBOURG         ST. MICHEL
                   ST. JEAN SAVERNE
SARREBOURG         SAVERNE

N

ROCHE DE DABO
EGENTHAL
                   STRASBOURG

LE DONON           BOERSCH
LA BROQUE
                   LANDSBERG
NEUNTELSTEIN
STE ODILE
                   DAMBACH
HAUT KOENIGSBOURG
                   RIBEAUVILLE
RIQUEWIHR
                   COLMAR

GERARDMER    COL
             DE SCHLUCHT
                   SOULTZBACH
             PETIT
             BALLON    COL DE BOENLESGRAB
             LAUTENBACH
    GRAND
    BALLON
ST. MAURICE
    BALLON
    D'ALCACE
                   CERNAY
GIROMAGNY    MARSEVAUX
                   MULHOUSE

BELFORT

RHINE

0   10   20   30   40   50   60
KILOMETRES

BASEL

# TOUR 7
# Eastern France—A Tour of the Vosges

'Why hop ye so, ye high hills?'    *Psalms*

---

| | |
|---|---|
| Distance: | 622km (385 miles). |
| Provinces: | Alsace-Lorraine and Vosges. |
| Maps: | I.G.N. Carte Touristique No. 104. Michelin Regional 1:200,000 Nos. 242, 243. |
| Guidebooks: | Michael Shaw, *Eastern France*, (Spurbooks). |
| Getting there: | By air to Strasbourg. |
| | By rail via Paris (Est) to Strasbourg or Sarrebourg. |
| Time required: | Two, or three weeks. |

**INTRODUCTION** By now, someone will be seeking a tour which also offers something in the nature of a physical challenge. This can be found, among unsurpassed scenery, in the green and hilly reaches of the Vosges. As you can see from a look at any topographic map, the Vosges mountains separate (or unite) the two ancient provinces of Alsace and Lorraine, which lie just inside France on the Western bank of the Rhine.

This has been a disputed territory for centuries. The Germans claimed it as spoils of war after defeating France in 1870. This provided one of the causes of the Great War after which it returned to France, only to be repossessed by the Germans in 1940, to revert finally to France in 1945. After all this it is not surprising that the region, although certainly French, has many Germanic overtones, notably in the placenames; Koenigsbourg, Bodenviller, Birkenwald, to mention but a few.

This tour begins in the town of Saverne, which can be easily reached from either Strasbourg or the rail junction at Sarrebourg. Saverne lies in the main gap of the Vosges range separating the Vosges du Nord from the more extensive southern hills. For my money the southern Vosges are also more attractive, but the north does offer the Parc Naturel Regional des Vosges du Nord, which runs up to the German frontier.

A word about gearing: this tour will involve a lot of hill climbing and so at least one 'granny' gear, of 30 inches or less, is highly advisable, certainly for loaded cycle-camping tours. The mountains or *ballons* as they are called locally, run up to 1525m or more and the climbs can be both long and steep. It would help to get tour fit before the start. Accommodation is no problem as there are plenty of hotels, youth hostels and gîtes d'étape, the latter often run by the local walking club, the Club Vosgian.

Strasbourg, home of the European Parliament, is an attractive city with many canals, and a fine Gothic cathedral, well worth a visit on a day's break from this demanding tour.

\* \* \*

From Saverne head north to St-Jean-Saverne and St-Michel then take minor roads as one should do whenever possible, into the Parc. The best route across the park is through Neuwiller to Weiterswiller and then in open country below the forest to Ingwiller (27km). Here turn left onto the D919 for Wimmenau, then north on the D181 up to the viewpoint at Lichtenberg, which has a fine castle in a region full of fine castles. From here minor roads lead north across the park to the town of Bitche, (27km) which makes a good ending to the first day.

Returning towards the south, first go west a little on the N62 before turning south on the D37 and up to the Pierre des 12 Apôtres near Kohlhutte and then down to the D919 at Wingen. From there the very minor D135 leads to the church and castle of La Petite Pierre, and so still by minor roads to the western side of the Vosges gap at Phalsbourg (30km). This section of the tour will take two days at a moderate pace and set you up for the more extensive wandering in the southern Vosges. Luckily the hills get higher as they move south, so the legs will be at least a little stronger when the long climbs begin.

Leave Phalsbourg for the south, turning off after 5km down the valley of the Zorn, a scenic route, and up to the Roche de Dabo (14km). This road winds and climbs with the occasional descent to Engenthal (12km) where a really good route, the minor D244, leads south under the Schneeberg (960m) which, as the name implies, is usually snow-covered in winter. It leads on across empty country to Le Donon (29km). If you picnic anywhere along this road beware of the fire risk and do not smoke. The pull up the Col du Donon (1009m) is a worthwhile climb for the views at the top are immense, across the Vosges and even across the Rhine to the Black Forest of Germany. From the Col enjoy the descent into the valley of the Bruche, to La Broque. Over the river lies the Reisling wine country, so cross the main road and take the D130, wandering south and east, past Neuntelstein, Ste. Odile and down to join the *Route des Vins* at Boersch, where the road turns south. Note this

*Route*, for the Vosges region is full of Routes and we shall follow a number of them on this tour. They always take in the most attractive places and are worthy of attention. This road which the Route des Vins has adopted, runs between the hills of the Vosges and the Rhine plain, through villages devoted entirely to the grape, but luckily it leads to some most attractive places; Landsberg, Dambach, and the classic Vosges castle at Haut-Koenigsbourg (45km). This region is full of castles, a relic of

The Fortress of Haut–Koenigsbourg

the frontier wars, so if like me you enjoy castles, you are in for a feast. Koenigsbourg has high walls and pointed towers, a splendid pile.

Continue on the Route des Vins, and visit Ribeauville (20km) and after a very necessary diversion to lovely Riquewihr, a centre for Reisling and Traminer wines, to Colmar. Colmar hardly seems like a French town at all, but rather more a German one, with storks' nests heaped untidily on every possible ledge, tower or steeple. There is a youth hostel here and many hotels, and this town, like Strasbourg, would be a good place to take a day out of the saddle, a very pleasant and picturesque place to stay.

South and west of Colmar the high hills begin, and we are leaving the fairly placid Route des Vins for the high, hard and breezy expanses of the *Route des Crêtes* (crests). Head west, leaving early before the traffic builds up on the fairly main D417, down the valley of the Fecht to Soulzbach, where we turn south and start to gain height. This road, the D2, climbs steadily to the Col de Boenlesgrab, at 865m (about 2600ft). Leave the bikes concealed hereabouts and try the short, steep walk up to the Petit Ballon (1267m).

After this enjoy a long swing down to Lautenbach and take the road south and east to Cernay (40km) at the start of the Route des Crêtes. The Route des Crêtes covers much of the high ground from Cernay, north to Belmont, and includes most but by no means all of the beautiful high country of the Vosges. In winter this is ski-country, noted especially for cross-country skiing, and so the little villages all have a ski-school and plenty of small hotels. Follow the Route from Cernay up (25km) to the Grand Ballon at 1424m, the highest point in the Vosges. From here on a good day you can see the distant Alps. Follow the Route des Crêtes to the Col de Schlucht, and there turn west to Gérardmer (45km), which you can reach in one full day. But you might like to linger on such a splendid Route and split this journey from Cernay to Gérardmer into two days and enjoy the views at leisure.

Gérardmer is the place for a rest. There is a vast lake surrounded by campsites where you can swim, boat or simply sunbathe, before setting off south yet again, across the southern Vosges for Belfort. Again, a really early start might be advisable because the first 40km are on a main road with plenty of climbing, and a full morning will be needed before the turn off for the Ballon d'Alsace appears at St. Maurice. From here it is a long, steep 10km climb up to the Ballon but the reward is a spectacular view and a long, winding staircase descent to Giromagny and so to Belfort (32km). There is a rail spur to Belfort at Giromagny and this comes in useful after a visit to Belfort, a superb fortified town, the only one to resist the advancing Germans in 1870, well worth a night stop and an evening's wander round the narrow streets.

Time will now be pressing, so take the rail spur back to Giromagny, and then head east on the D12 to Marsavaux to pick up yet another Route, the *Route Joffre*. Marshal Joffre commanded the French Armies in the early years of the Great War and this attractive road leads us back again to Cernay (50km).

From Cernay the tourist has two choices. If time is really short there are trains for the north and good connections for Strasbourg. Time permitting, the ride back to the starting point through the vineyards is fast, and now with strong legs, fairly easy. If more hills are required, or there is time in hand, the railway could take you up the valley of the Thur to St. Nicolas, to climb again to the Col de Schlucht and the northern section of the Route des Crêtes.

I suspect though, that the tour as outlined above, terminating at the station in Cernay, will prove enough. The Vosges cannot be rushed and a 60km-a-day-average will prove quite sufficient and still allow for those detours and diversions to which travellers in the Vosges are particularly susceptible. The area does have good, short rail links which are not too common in mountain regions and are probably due here to the area's winter purpose as a ski zone. Use the railway if time gets short and you will be able to see a great deal of the Vosges. Enough, I am sure, to make you want to come again.

View over the Wine country near Riquewihr

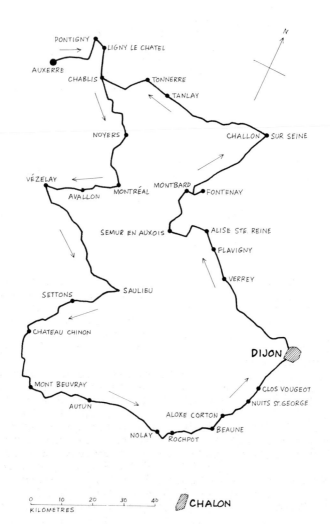

PONTIGNY

LIGNY LE CHATEL

AUXERRE

CHABLIS

TONNERRE

TANLAY

NOYERS

CHALLON

SUR SEINE

VÉZELAY

MONTBARD

FONTENAY

AVALLON

MONTRÉAL

SEMUR EN AUXOIS

ALISE STE. REINE

FLAVIGNY

VERREY

SETTONS

SAULIEU

CHATEAU CHINON

MONT BEUVRAY

DIJON

CLOS VOUGEOT

NUITS ST. GEORGE

AUTUN

ALOXE CORTON

NOLAY

ROCHPOT

BEAUNE

0   10   20   30   40

KILOMETRES

CHALON

N

# TOUR 8
# A Tour in Burgundy

**'The best way to suppose what may come, is to remember the past'.**
**George Savile,** *On Experience*

---

| | |
|---|---|
| Distance: | 761km (470 miles). |
| Province: | Burgundy (Côte d'Or, Yonne, Morvan). |
| Maps: | I.G.N. Carte Touristique No. 118. Michelin Regional 1:200,000 Nos. 243 and 238. |
| Guidebooks: | Neil Lands, *Burgundy*, (Spurbooks). |
| | Robert Speight, *Companion Guide to Burgundy*, (Collins). |
| Ports: | Any Channel port via Paris. |
| Time required: | Two weeks. |

**INTRODUCTION** It might be as well to declare an interest and say here and now that Burgundy is one of my favourite French provinces. It is rich in history, wine, good food and splendid scenery, all of which interest me. Compared with such popular places as Normandy or Provence it is virtually unknown. Last but by no means least, it is not too far away, and easily reached via Paris.

Burgundy was once one of the mightiest dukedoms in Europe, and flourished notably in the reign of the four Valois dukes, who ruled there between 1364 and 1477, spanning the rich period of the high Middle Age up to the dawn of the Renaissance. That century has left Burgundy with a great legacy of historic and artistic treasures. It is a place to wander in, not a place to rush about, and to get about in Burgundy and see what it has to offer, a bicycle is ideal. Today, Burgundy has shrunk to the pre-Valois boundaries. It begins in the north at Montereau, just south of Paris, where one Valois duke, John the Fearless, was murdered in 1419 and runs from there a long way south into the wine-drenched Beaujolais. The terrain is moderate everywhere, but often quite hilly, getting fairly rugged in the Morvan Regional Park between Vézelay and the town of Autun and in the warmer regions of the south, but normal gearing will be sufficient if the rider is moderately fit.

It is possible to ride into Burgundy from Paris, crossing the boundary river, the Yonne, at Montereau and following that river south. Burgundy is a big, straggling province, so what follows is a tour *in* Burgundy, rather than a tour *of* Burgundy. One cannot hope to see it all in two weeks, but this tour begins at a classic Burgundian centre, the town of Auxerre.

\* \* \*

Walter Pater said that Auxerre—pronounced 'Aussaire'—was

Clocktower Street, Auxerre

the prettiest town in France; certainly it is very attractive, with lots of narrow streets, Gothic churches and a beautiful river and canal front where the Yonne and the Canal du Nivernais flow into the city.

Leave the town by the D104, heading north-east on a scenic route for the Cistercian abbey at Pontigny (30km) which once sheltered Thomas à Becket, a pleasant opening ride and a worthwhile sight with which to begin a tour of Burgundy. After a stop here, turn south through Ligny-le-Châtel for Chablis (15km), a famous centre for an excellent wine. Don't miss the Church of St. Martin, where the door is covered with horseshoes, nailed up by medieval knights as votive offerings.

From Chablis continue south along the river Serein to Noyers (20km) a little gem of a place, all half-timbered houses, well worth a visit and very photogenic, a good place to stay. A scenic route continues out of Noyers, still following the Serein, for most of the way to the little hill-top town of Montréal (22km). You may be tempted to miss Montréal, but don't; ride up the narrow steep streets to the little church on the hill which contains some marvellous and very rare sixteenth century carvings, a little-known place, like so much of Burgundy, but one not to be missed.

From Montréal a short ride to the west leads to the town of Avallon (19km). Avallon has plenty of hotels and campsites, but it lies on the main N6 Route National, and tends to get drowned by traffic in summer. It is however an historic town worth exploring before riding out to one of the great places of France, a real must for any traveller, the town and pilgrim church at Vézelay (13km). You must allow at least half a day to enjoy Vézelay, the place where Bernard of Clairvaux preached the Second Crusade, and one of the four departure points for pilgrims heading to the shrine of St-James at Compostela.

Vézelay stands at the northern edge of the Parc Naturel Regional du Morvan, and the next two to three days can be spent riding slowly across this wooded, hilly and beautiful region to Saulieu, to the great lake at Settons, and up to the heights at Château Chinon and to the top of Mont Beuvray where, once upon a time, Julius Caesar and Mark Antony spent a chilly winter. The Morvan is full of tempting minor roads, and my route across it, with frequent diversions, took 217km, and three days. I could happily have taken longer.

Emerging from the park at Autun, which has Roman ruins, a fine cathedral and an interesting museum, an early start and a quick 32km takes us to Nolay on the edge of the wine country of the Côte de Beaune. Nolay, like Noyers, is an attractive little town full of medieval buildings, a good night stop, and from here the scenic route takes us to Rochpot (6km) which has a great medieval château-fort, with one of those colourful, glittering Burgundian roofs . . . and so to the wine country.

A 'côte' is an escarpment, and there are two notable 'côtes' in the Burgundy region of the Côte d'Or; the Côte de Beaune which lies south of that town, and the Côte de Nuits, which lies to the north of it. Both are famous for their Burgundy wines, and every village will seem familiar from your well-remembered wine lists: Meursault, Pommard, Puligny, Montrachet, Nuits St-Georges, and many more. There is a slightly wandering

A typical porched church in Burgundy

scenic route which follows the côtes, above and to the east of the main north-south road which is traffic-filled and best avoided. The journey from Nolay to Dijon, the present capital of Burgundy, by minor roads, is a pleasant route, and totals some 80km.

Stop in Beaune for at least half a day, to visit the marvellous Hotel-Dieu, see the wine museum, visit a few caves, and drink a little wine. A cyclist cannot carry much of the local vintage but a little sampling (*dégustastion*) can be fun. Ride out to Aloxe-Corton, Nuits St-Georges and see the Château at Clos-Vougeot. Arriving in Dijon, Dijon of the dukes, visit their palace which contains their magnificent tombs, see the cathedral and wander in the narrow backstreets. You can also buy some mustard!

From Dijon, head north on another minor road, the one which leads past the autodrome, where motor races are held, and on the D10 to Verrey and the town of Flavigny (51km). Then on to the little town of Alise-Ste-Reine. Here Julius Caesar defeated the Gallic warlord, Vercingetorix in 52 BC. There are three Romano-Gallic museums in the town and the shrine and well of Ste Reine. To the west, at some 15km, lies the mighty walled city of Semur-en-Auxois, and to the north of that, Montbard (18km). Another very worthwhile stop is the well-preserved abbey of Fontenay.

From here, if time permits, go north yet again, for 33km to Châtillon-sur-Seine. Not many people visit Châtillon, which is a pity, for the small museum there contains the fabulous golden Gallic treasure of Vix. At Châtillon, it might be as well to end the tour with a good dinner and head north for Paris and the boat home, but if there is still time in hand, then there is still good touring country to the west, through Tanlay and Tonnerre, into Chablis to pick up a little wine, and so at last, after some 85km, into Auxerre, where this journey began, and ends.

\* \* \*

Burgundy, as you will have noticed, is a province full of interesting sights and many fascinating places. Writing a book about it, I once took a solid month touring by car to visit only the larger places, and it is idle to pretend that one can see all of this rich historic province in one visit. This tour has not visited the Beaujolais, the Nivernais or the pleasant places along the river Saône, but it will, I feel sure, give an interesting and enjoyable holiday and whet the traveller's appetite for this delightful and underrated province and, after all, you can always come again.

# TOUR 9
# A Ride Round Paris

**'For you the City, thus I turn my back:
There is a world elsewhere.'**
### *Shakespeare, Coriolanus*

---

| | |
|---|---|
| Distance: | 714km (445 miles). |
| Province: | Ile-de-France. |
| Maps: | I.G.N. Carte Touristique No. 103 Ile-de-France; Champagne. Michelin Regional 1:200,000 No. 237 and No. 170 Environs de Paris (spécial cyclotourisme) 1:100,000. |
| Guidebooks: | Ian Dunlop, *The Companion Guide to the Ile-de-France*, (Collins). |
| | Marion Deschamps, *The Ile-de-France*, (Foulis). |
| Getting there: | By ferry to the Channel ports of Dieppe, Le Havre or Boulogne, then by train or bike to Beauvais. |
| Time required: | Two weeks. |

**INTRODUCTION**  Any tour, however pleasant, is all the better for a theme. The theme of this tour in the Ile-de-France is art, architecture and history; if you like such things you will like this tour. If not, not.

It ought to be explained that some 1300 years ago, and indeed up to the early years of the thirteenth century, the king of the Franks or French, was by no means King of France. He was simply *primus inter pares*, first among equals, and ruled directly only in a wide but contained tract of land around Paris, circled by several rivers, the Marne, the Oise and the Eure, and known therefore as the Ile-de-France. The name endures; Charles de Gaulle Airport is at Roissy-en-France.

Medieval kings needed forests. Not only was hunting their sole recreation but they also needed fresh meat from the game to feed their court in winter and, as a result, the Ile-de-France was and remains heavily forested, and is still full of deer. It is also littered with the splendid palaces of the kings and the nobility of France. Many of these palaces are now museums and the collections they contain are rare and magnificent. To see them is the object of this journey.

There are no less than 118 museums in the Ile-de-France, but I do not propose visiting them all. With that number available, one can afford to be selective. If you enjoy beautiful things then this is the tour for you, and the cycling through the forests and over the fertile farmland is also very pleasant. Normal gears will be adequate and there is plenty of accommodation.

Perhaps a word ought to be said here about security. Leaving all your traps on the bike and then disappearing into a museum for a couple of hours can be risky. I recommend early starts, morning rides and then leaving your cycle and possessions in some security, either in that day's hotel or at the lunchtime restaurant, which, after the meal, will usually be helpful. Carpark attendants will frequently be obliging and keep an eye on your bike for five francs. As always, a good lock and chain and full insurance are advisable.

\* \* \*

This tour ought to begin at Sceaux, in the inner suburbs of Paris, where the château contains the Musée de l'Ile-de-France, which sets the history of the region out in detail, but for reasons of time we begin at Beauvais, a cathedral city, easily reached from Le Havre or Dieppe. A visit to the cathedral there, though pleasant, will not delay you for long. Then ride out, to the east and south to Chantilly (43km). A pleasant minor road, the D44, leads off after Noailles and the ride is an attractive one, through forested country down to the river Oise. The castle of Chantilly is quite beautiful, the perfect introduction to the architectural glories of the Ile-de-France. It dates from the early seventeenth century, stands in a lake and contains many rare treasures, including that fifteenth-century masterpiece, The Duc de Barri's Book of Hours *Les Trés Riches Heures*. The Château was built by the princes of Condé, and take note of the large and lavish stables. One of the owners of Chantilly believed in reincarnation, thinking that he would return to earth as a horse, and so he built stable accommodation suitable for a former prince.

From Chantilly take the minor road through Avilly St. Léonard to Senlis (12km), an old cathedral city with a hunting museum full of relics of the chase, and then go north-east through Ognon, Raray, and St. Pierre, across the forest of Compiègne, on minor roads and forest tracks to Compiègne itself, (49km). Compiègne has various attractions and much history. Joan of Arc was captured here by the Burgundians in 1430, and later sold to the English. A little outside the city, in a clearing in the forest, stands a railway carriage where the

1918 Armistice was signed, thus ending the Great War. To be exact this is not the original carriage, but a similar one. In 1940 the Germans insisted that the French surrender should take place in the original carriage, after which it was burned, so this is a replacement.

The chief glory of Compiègne though, is the vast palace, a favourite home of the Emperor, Napoleon III and his Empress Eugenie, a splendid pile, so, with one thing and another, there is plenty to see and do in historic Compiègne.

South-east of here, across the forest via a minor scenic route which runs north of the main road, lies the fine, if much restored, medieval castle of Pierrefonds (10km). After a look at the castle and its superb setting, take the road south through Morienval, which has a splendid church, and so to Crépy-en-Valois (16km), a pleasant, dreamy little place, once noted for the skill of the local archers.

From Crépy, the next sight lies a long way to the south, across the farmlands of Valois and Brie. Pass through Betz (10km) to the valley of the river Ourcq and follow the river south to La Ferté and Jouarre (40km). Our objective is the walled city of Provins, just north of the Seine, which guards the eastern gateway to Paris. There are plenty of minor roads across the country, so allow a full day for this trip of some 60km. Provins has some splendid medieval fortifications and one huge tower, a magnificent relic of the past. There are also several hotels and this is a good place to stay.

The Château at Fontainebleau

After Provins, drop down to the Seine and follow the river west, skirting Montereau and press on to Moret-sur-Loing (45km), a picturesque little town with a fine old bridge, and then go north through the forest to Fontainbleau, one of the great tourist attractions of the region. The palace is huge and was the favourite residence of French kings before the building of Versailles. To see Fontainebleau will take at least half a day, after which it would be a good idea to ride north to see another magnificent château, Vaux-le-Vicomte, built with money stolen from the Royal treasury by Louis XIV's chancellor, Nicolas Fouquet. Fouquet employed the great architects and craftsmen of the period, Le Vau, Le Brun and Le Nôtre, in the building of Vaux, but he enjoyed its magnificence for a very short time. Louis XIV had him arrested for peculation and he died in prison. But see Vaux, the classic French château.

Ride south from here, through Melun and back into the forest to Barbizon, a great place for painters, and on to little Milly-le-Fôret to see the chapel of St-Blaise which has a unique herb garden and frescoes by Jean Cocteau. You could happily stay the night in Milly.

Then we embark on another cross-country wander west to the great château at Rambouillet, once a royal home, now the summer residence of the President of France. By minor roads, through St-Cyr-sur-Dourdon, this is a pleasant ride of around 80km, a good day's run. From Rambouillet it makes sense to visit Versailles, which is only 30km away to the north and easily reached by train. If you should decide to ride, travel by the valley of Chevreuse and Port Royal. To see Versailles and all that it contains will take a full day.

North-west of Rambouillet lies the town of Montfort l'Amaury, once the seat of that Simon de Montfort, a knight of the Ile de France who established the English Parliament and was killed at Evesham. After visiting Montfort turn south for an easy ride across the plain of the Beauce to the cathedral city of Chartres (53km). To get this close and not see Chartres would be a terrible shame, for the cathedral there is the most splendid example of the Gothic style, towering over the roofs of this hilltop town it draws the traveller on across the plain.

Leave Chartres by the scenic road along the river Eure to Nogent-le-Roi (27km), and then across country to Anet (28km) where the little château was once the home of Henry II's mistress, Diane de Poitiers; it is a gem, well worth a visit.

After Anet turn north, wandering across country to the town of Vernon (46km) on the Seine. At nearby Giverny (3km) see the home and water-gardens of the painter Claude Monet, stopping for the night at La Roche Guyon (14km).

From La Roche Guyon follow the valley of the river Epte,

which marks the boundary between Normandy and the Ile-de-France, through the country of the Vexin to Gisors (30km), which has a well-preserved medieval castle and, with a final 35km completed, arrive at last back in the city of Beauvais and the end of this journey.

*   *   *

This tour has encircled Paris, and with that delightful city so near it might be a good idea to take a train at any station in the Ile-de-France for a day or an evening in the '*Ville Lumière*'. This ride can be cut at various points and riders returning via Le Havre can pick up a train at Vernon.

# TOUR 10
# A Tour of the Cévennes
## 'The great affair is to move . . .'
### *R. L. Stevenson,* Travels With a Donkey in the Cévennes

---

| | |
|---|---|
| Distance: | 527km (327 miles). |
| Provinces: | Auvergne, Languedoc-Roussillon. |
| Maps: | I.G.N. Carte Touristique Nos. 111 Auvergne and 114 Pyrénées-Languedoc. Michelin 1:200,000 No. 239 Auvergne-Limousin and Regional No. 240 Languedoc-Roussillon. |
| Guidebooks: | Robert Louis Stevenson, *Travels with a Donkey in the Cévennes.* Neil Lands, *Languedoc-Roussillon,* (Spurbooks). |
| Getting there: | By train via Paris, and Clermont-Ferrand to Le Puy. Home: by train or by air from Montpellier. |
| Time required: | Two to three weeks. |

**INTRODUCTION** This route essentially follows the one taken by the Scottish writer, Robert Louis Stevenson and his donkey, Modestine, in 1878, a classic walk then and now, across a little-known part of France. Since *then*, however, many of the tracks they followed have been metalled over and so although the roads are often very minor indeed, the route is cyclable in all but a few places, which can be skirted without difficulty.

One difficulty which may exist is the one posed by the time problem, which inevitably arises when cycles are sent on long trans-France journeys without the riders. My advice in this case is that the cycle be sent overnight to Clermont-Ferrand or St-Flour, collected there and taken on a code 40 *vélos en baggage à main* to Le Puy.

Even so, allow at least two days to the start line; if you leave the U.K. on Friday, it may well be Monday before you ride out of Le Monastier-sur-Gazielle. On the way home the same rule will apply; send the cycle ahead from Montpellier to the Gare-de-Lyon in Paris and ride it across to the Gare-du-Nord or St-Lazare, taking it on the train with you to the Channel coast.

This is one reason why I recommend allowing three weeks for this trip, which covers some of the most beautiful country in France. The region is hilly, so at least one low gear of 30in or less will be useful.

This trip begins where Stevenson's did, in the little town of Le Monastier-sur-Gazielle, south-east of Le Puy. There is a small obelisk commemorating his walk, outside the Post Office, and we will leave from there.

\* \* \*

From Le Monastier take the minor road to Goudet (13km) and have coffee in the Hotel de la Loire by the bridge. Stevenson stayed here and the present owner, M. Senac, is a direct descendant of the hotelier who entertained him.

Then ride west, across the main road at Costaros, to Le Bouchet-St Nicolas, 16km, and then south on minor roads to Pradelles (24km). According to legend the statue of the Virgin in the church at Pradelles 'performs many miracles, though she be of wood', and the town itself is attractive.

Pass through to Langogne (9km) and take the minor road, directly south, for Les Pradels and then down a steep hill into Luc, picking up the D906 for Rogleton and the Monastery of Notre-Dame-des-Neiges, Our Lady of the Snows, another Stevenson stop. Cyclists are welcome to stop here but you will need sleeping bags and may have to sleep in the barn. The monks will feed you for a modest sum and their welcome is always warm. On arrival ask for the *Père Hôteliére*.

Leaving the monastery, pass through La Bastide-Puylaurant and take the road, as Stevenson did, for Chassarades (12km) turning south there to climb the road over the Montagne du Goulet (1497m). The track descends steeply after Les Alpiers into Le Bleymard. The distance is not great, at around 12km but the climb is steep and leads directly down to another, for the trail leads out of Le Bleymard and up over Mont Lozère (1699m) into the Parc National des Cévennes. Then you go down to the infant Tarn at Le Pont-de-Montvert (23km) again not far but with a steep climb to the Col de Finiels (1541m), for some marvellous views as far as the distant Mediterranean on a clear day.

At Pont-de-Montvert the trail turns west for 21km, to the pretty town of Florac, and here we leave Stevenson's route to turn directly south for the Col du Rey (12km) and the northern end of the Corniche des Cévennes, which runs for 53km down to the end of Stevenson's journey, at the town of St-Jean-du-Gard.

It would be a good idea to spend a day or two at St-Jean, either resting, walking in the hills, or riding out on parts of

Stevenson's route, to St-Germaine-de-Calberte, or Moissac-Vallée Française. This is a lovely part of France, and worth exploring.

The Causse Mejean above the Tarn

Leaving St-Jean, head up the river Gardon towards the loom of Mont Aigoual (1362m), up and down the hills to Vallerauge, Le Esperou and into Le Vigan, (106km). This is a long, hard ride, best taken in two stages. From Le Vigan go south and descend into the vast natural amphitheatre of the Cirque de Navacelles, (27km) which is a fascinating place, in spite of the need to climb up out of it again. From here take the road to St-Guilhem-le-Désert, a quiet and lovely village, and then on to the Pont du Diable at St-Jean-de-Fos for a swim in the Hérault before continuing to Gignac (49km). From here it is only 30km to Montpellier, where the bikes can be entrained for Paris while the riders take a day to explore and enjoy this elegant university city, or get even browner on the nearby beaches of the Languedoc littoral.

This ride is not too long, at around the 500km mark, but it will be hot, the hills are steep, and the countryside is so beautiful that the temptation to stop will always be there . . . and why resist it? This is a trip which I have done twice and intend to do again.

ANGOULEME

ST. EMILLION    CAPET    LA ROCHE CHALAIS
                                ST. AULAYE
PETIT PALAIS
CASTILLON LA BATAILLE
CHATEAU DE MONTAGNE          RIBERAC

                              BOURDEILLES
STE. FOY                      BRANTOME
                              CHANCELADE
                              PERIGUEX

BERGERAC
EYMET    MONTBAZILLAC
ISSIGEAC                      CINGLE DE TREMOLAT
         LALINDE             TREMOLAT
VILLERÉAL  CADOUIN          PONT COUDE
                            LES EYZIES    MONTIGNAC
         MONTPAZIER
BIRON                       BEYNAC
         CASTELNAUD         SARLAT
                           MONTFORT        BRIVE LA
         DOMME                             GAILLARDE

                                           TURENNE
                           SOUILLAC
              LA TRAYNE            MARTEL
         ROCAMADOUR              MONTVALENT
                                   DORDOGNE

                           ISLE

0    10   20   30   40   50   60   70   80   90
KILOMETRES

# TOUR 11
# A Tour of the Dordogne
## 'The past is a foreign country, they do things differently there.'
### *L. P. Hartley, The Go-between*

---

| | |
|---|---|
| Distance: | 620km (385 miles). |
| Province: | Midi-Pyréneés (Périgord). |
| Maps: | I.G.N. Carte Touristique No. 110; Michelin 1:200,000 Nos. 233, Poitou-Charentes and 235 Midi-Pyrénées. |
| Guidebooks: | Neil Lands, *A Visitor's Guide to the Dordogne*, (Moorland). |
| | Freda White, *Three Rivers of France*, (Faber). |
| | Michelin Green Guide, *The Dordogne*. |
| Getting there: | By air via Bordeaux. |
| | By rail via Paris, Limoges and Périgueux. |
| Time required: | Two to three weeks. |

**INTRODUCTION** There can be no real need to sing the praises of the Dordogne to the British traveller. This is a beautiful part of France, and it has been justly popular with the British for the last 20 years. For this reason, parts of it have become a trifle tourist-infested, and this tour therefore aims to take the cycletourist to some of those places in the Dordogne where the other kind don't (often) go. It can get very hot in the Dordogne during the summer months, and the terrain, if never mountainous, is usually hilly. In spite of the heat and the hills though, normal gearing will be adequate.

This tour circles the *département* of the Dordogne and does not merely follow the river which gives the *département* its name. The area is notably rich in Anglo-French history and as part of the ancient duchy of Aquitaine once belonged to the English kings until they were finally expelled from France in 1453; those who love history will find a lot of it in the Dordogne. Much of it will be familiar from our own history books. The area also contains the prehistoric sites at Lascaux, the pilgrim town of Rocamadour, many castles, and the *bastide* towns, all beautiful, all historic. It is also noted for fine food and wine, so that whatever you seek in France, this place can provide it.

Our travels begin in the capital of the old county of Périgord, the city of Périgueux.

\*　\*　\*

Périgueux stands on the river Isle, and is an attractive city, with a curious cathedral, St-Front, crowned with little minarets. A visit to the large departmental Syndicat d'Initiative in the rue President Wilson will provide much useful current information on the area before you leave, heading north, past the abbey at Chancelade, which is well worth a visit, to two lovely little places which must not be missed, Bourdeilles (25km) and nearby Brantôme (10km). Both stand on the river Drôme, which gives each place a fine river setting. From Brantôme return down the D78/D710 to Ribérac (37km) to St-Aulaye (20km) and through La Roche-Chalais (12km) to little Capet, where we turn south on a scenic route, through Petit Palais to the wine town of St Emilion (35km). St Emilion is a very old town, well established in Roman times, and with a charter originally granted by the English King John, who is better known to the French as Jean-Sans-Terre, John Lackland. St Emilion is one of the great towns of the claret country, a good place to stay. It is surrounded by vineyards and the châteaux of the various growers, many of which can be visited.

Leave St Emilion for the town of Castillon-la-Bataille (12km) on the banks of the Dordogne. The battle in question was the last major action of the Hundred Years War, when the French defeated the English earl, John Talbot, 'great marshal to our lord Henry VI, of all his wars within the realm of the French'. There is a memorial to Talbot on the banks of the river, and various others on the site of the battle.

A brief trip east along the busy main road leads up to the château of Montaigne (8km) which was once the home of the writer, Michel de Montaigne, who invented the essay as a literary form and was the friend and counsellor of Henry of Navarre. The tower in which he wrote is still intact and exactly as he describes it in his memoirs.

From Montaigne, avoiding the traffic on the main route east up the river by using minor roads, head west to Ste-Foy (18km) and then on the north bank to Bergerac (25km).

Bergerac, like most of the towns hereabouts, is a wine centre, producing good, hearty reds, but it is also a centre for the French home-grown tobacco industry, and there is a Musée du Tabac in the town centre. At Bergerac turn south, across the vineyards into the country of the *bastides*, which are small, walled, fortified towns, built in the thirteenth century by both the French and the English to garrison the disputed marches of Aquitaine. They are very beautiful and just the right distances apart to provide perfect stages on a cycletour.

Head past the Château at Montbazillac, which produces a sweet white wine, to the first bastide, Eymet (39km). From here the route wanders east to Issigac (20km) and to two splendid bastides, the best of them all, Villeréal and Montpazier. On the way between the two do not fail to visit the mighty castle of Biron, for the setting is superb.

From Montpazier ride north to Cadouin (16km) and see the church which once contained the famous relic of the Holy Shroud, and cross the river at Lalinde (14km) to make the steep climb up the north bank to the viewpoint which overlooks the great sweep of the river called the Cingle de Trémolat (25km). The view from up here is marvellous, and apart from that the climb is rewarded by fine descents down to Trémolat, which has a huge fortified church. Follow the river upstream to the 'Elbow Bridge', the Pont Coude (7km) where the river Vézère flows into the main Dordogne.

A trip up the Vézère cannot be missed, for not only is the countryside very beautiful, but this valley also contains some rare, almost unique relics of the world's prehistoric past, at Les Eyzies and Lasçaux. Visit the Museum of Prehistory at Les Eyzies (16km) which will tell the story, and then press on up the valley to Montignac and Lascaux (24km). The painted caves at Lascaux were only discovered in 1940, but the atmospheric changes since caused by crowds of visitors have eroded the

Place de la Halle, Domme

paintings, until the caves have had to be closed except to very occasional visitors and academics. However, a full-scale detailed replica, Lascaux II, has recently been opened, which is almost as good and well worth seeing.

From Montignac ride directly south to the beautiful medieval town of Sarlat (25km) a real gem of a place, ideal to wander round on a soft summer evening, and the gateway to the castle country of the Dordogne. Stay the night and at least half a day

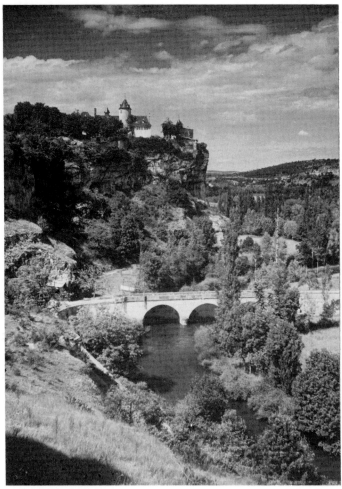

View of Belcastel

in Sarlat before riding south to see the great castles at Beynac (21km) and Castelnaud (10km) high above the valley, with the classic Château of Feyrac close by, and then take the steep and winding road which leads up to the beautiful bastide of Domme (35km).

Domme is sure to be full of visitors, but even cluttered with crowds it cannot be spoiled. The town is a dream of golden stone, picked out with the red of dark geraniums, and the view over the valley from the ramparts is one of the finest in this part of France.

Leaving Domme, sweep down to the river once again, and turn east out of Périgord, into the neighbouring province of Quercy, past the fairy-tale castle at Montfort to Souillac (32km). Crossing the river at La Trayne, see Belcastel high on the bluff, before taking the scenic route across to the pilgrim town of Rocamadour (28km), a fantastic sight for the houses there cling to the side of the gorge. There is a lot to see in Rocamadour, including fine old houses and the Shrine of the Black Virgin, but that first view is the best of it.

At Rocamadour turn north, crossing the river yet again near Montvalent, and climb up to the Causse de Martel, crossing it to the little town of Martel, which is well worth a night stop. Heading north from here to Brive, the main N20 road should be avoided at all costs. It is usually all a-roar with traffic, lorries, caravans, and fast cars; so take the minor scenic route D20/D8/D38, past the last great castle at Turenne, and descend at last into Brive-la-Gaillarde (60km) and the end of this journey.

\* \* \*

This tour could be accomplished in two weeks if the tourist maintained an average of 80km (50 miles) per day, which is the mileage originally envisaged when planning most of the tours in this book. However, when actually on the tour the distractions which cut the average down or add to the distance, kept popping up.

A two-week tour really needs to start with a time-saving flight to Bordeaux. On most tours there are usually long linking sections which can be ridden in the morning, leaving the afternoons free for sightseeing and so cutting into the overall necessary mileage, but the Dordogne country is a place where there is something new to stop and exclaim at around almost every bend. It takes time to see and enjoy it all, so take your time and, if possible, at least three weeks of it.

# TOUR 12
# A Tour of the Basque Country

## 'The Basques are a little people, who dance at the foot of the Pyrénées.'
### *Voltaire*

---

| | |
|---|---|
| Distance: | 576km (360 miles). |
| Province: | Midi-Pyrénées (Pays Basque, Béarn). |
| Maps: | I.G.N. Carte Touristique No. 113 Pyrénées-Occidentales; Michelin Regional 1:200,000 No. 234. |
| Guidebooks: | Neil Lands, *The French Pyrénées*, (Spurbooks). |
| Getting there: | By air to Bordeaux and then to Bayonne by train. |
| | By rail via Paris and Bordeaux. |
| | By ferry to Santander in Spain and then to Bayonne via Hendaye. |
| Time required: | Two or three weeks. |

**INTRODUCTION** France is a very varied country and even the population is by no means homogenous. Use French as an adjective and you can add Catalans and Basques to a population which already includes Bretons, Normans, Auvergnats, and a good many more identifiable minorities. To those who know it well, this infinite variety is another of France's many attractions, another layer to the cake, and few parts are as varied, as attractive, or as interesting as the green and pleasant country of the Basques. The Basque country occupies the south-western corner of France and consists of three distinct districts, Soule, Sourde and Navarre, each a province of the old kingdom of Navarre which once straddled the Pyrénées.

The Basques are different and anyone entering one of these three provinces will notice the difference at once in both the architecture and in the people. The Basques have their own language, culture and traditions. They sing their own songs and they also dance, as Voltaire so tartly pointed out, notably the Fandango. Their country is a green and hilly one, even mountainous in parts, very attractive, and scattered with small villages and little towns. The first cycle ride I ever made in France took me to the Basque country and I remember the trip with considerable affection. It was different.

This tour will also include a little of the neighbouring county of Béarn, and since 'county' is an English term I should explain that where it exists in France it refers to a medieval lordship rather than to an administrative district. The medieval counts of Béarn contained and resisted the kings of Navarre, and the two regions provide the modern visitor with startling contrasts between the land of the French and the land of the Basques.

After the flat forest of the Landes has been crossed from Bordeaux which, if done on the bike, will take about a day, the region becomes hilly, but the hills are moderate and will present no real problems. This tour begins at Bayonne.

\* \* \*

Bayonne is one of those sparkling provincial French cities, full of cafes and winding streets, with a large Gothic cathedral, and an interesting Basque museum, which is a useful stop. The history and culture of the Basques is complex and a visit here will add greatly to the enjoyment and understanding of the trip which follows. That apart, Bayonne is an historic town credited with the invention of the bayonet, full of narrow streets and picturesque corners, very photogenic.

Main roads are always best avoided but take the one that leads south on a short ride to the coastal holiday resort of Biarritz (8km), an Edwardian-style town, once popular with our King Edward VII. It is now a great surfing centre and has excellent restaurants and good hotels. From Biarritz continue south, along the coast, a gentle introduction to this trip, through St-Jean-de-Luz to Hendaye (38km) on the Spanish frontier.

Turn east at Hendaye and pick up the minor roads, and travel on them inland on a tour through three pretty and very Basque villages, Ascain, Sare and Ainhoa (40km). The hills are steep but not too high, and the views are worth any effort. Between Ascain and Sare, at the Col de St-Ignace, take a side-trip on the little railway that climbs to the summit of La Rhune (900m) the high peak of the Basque foothills. From Ainhoa ride on to Combo-les-Bains, (15km), once the home of Edmond Rostand, author of *Cyrano de Bergerac*, a very Basque town. Keep a look out for pelota courts, and if a game is in progress, stop and watch this exciting and skilful sport.

From Cambo take the scenic road that leads south and east along the river Nive to the town of St-Jean-Pied-de-Port (34km) a major stop on the pilgrim road to Compostela, and a most attractive town. See the old street which leads down to the Church of Notre-Dame-du-Pont, and try a *jambon piperade*, a

Basque dish of ham, eggs and peppers, in any one of the restaurants by the bridge over the Nive.

From St-Jean ride out to the north, to St-Jean-le-Vieux and then on to Larceveau (16km) turning east here, for the Col d'Osquich and over the hills to Mauléon-Licharre (24km). Our route for the next day or so leads across the foothills of the Western Pyrénées, but these northern ramparts of the mountains are not too high, and each climb will have a rewarding descent. From Mauléon-Licharre, turn south up the valley of the Saison, past Gotein, where the pelota court is actually part of the church, very photogenic, and up towards the Haute Soule and the town of Tardets-Sorholus (16km). Turn east and follow the mountain road through Lanne, visiting Aramits, said to have been the home of Aramis, one of the Three Musketeers, and then a steep climb over into the valley of the Aspe (39km) for a real taste of the Hautes Pyrénées. This tour is not a mountain tour, so after a ride up the Aspe valley (26km) turn north for the town of Oloron-Ste-Marie (31km).

Oloron is a pretty place, divided by the Aspe, with two great churches. From here take the minor road, out of the Basque country for a while, to the city of Pau (31km) via Gan in the wine country of the Jurançon. Pau, like Bayonne, is a fine city and was the birthplace of one of France's most popular monarchs, Henry IV, of France and Navarre. From the Promenade overlooking the river, the Gave de Pau, there are fine views of the snow-tipped Pyrénées to the south.

Pau is the capital of Béarn and here, after days in the Basque country the traveller will be struck by the fact that he or she is once again back in France. These Basques are of course French Basques, and proud of it, but their homeland just a little way to the west of Pau is very clearly a different country, a contrast to the Gallic charms of elegant Pau.

Leaving Pau, follow the minor roads back to the Basque country (45km) on the south bank of the river, through Mourenx all the way west to Orthez, which is a medieval town with a great fortified bridge. From here our road lies south again, to two attractive towns, Salies-de-Béarn and Sauveterre-de-Béarn (31km) both of which are well worth a visit, with fine buildings and attractive *quartiers* to stroll around. Then ride a little further south to St-Palais (12km) and on through Garris across country to Bidache (27km) which has a huge, half-ruined castle. From here, again on minor roads, make a final wander west, through the green Basque countryside and so back to Bayonne (35km), and the end of the journey.

\* \* \*

This trip will show the tourist, and at a pleasant pace, one of the most delightful corners of France. The Basque country has great variety: high mountains as a backdrop, rolling hills in the foreground, fine towns and pretty, well-cared-for villages almost everywhere. This trip, while enjoyable in itself, will also be an appetiser for an extended tour in the Hautes Pyrénées further south. If you like to go somewhere different, then this is the place to go.

# TOUR 13
# Eastern Aquitaine

**'Tell me a story that nobody knows
And show me a country where nobody
goes.'** *Anon*

---

| | |
|---|---|
| Distance: | 554kms (345 miles). |
| Province: | Midi-Pyrénées. |
| Maps: | I.G.N. Carte Touristique No. 114. Pyrénées-Languedoc, and No. 111 Auvergne. Michelin Regional 1:200,000 No. 235 Midi-Pyrénées. |
| Guidebooks: | Neil Lands, *Beyond the Dordogne*, (Spurbooks). |
| Getting there: | By air, or rail via Paris, to Toulouse, then by rail to Albi. |
| Time required: | Two weeks. |

**INTRODUCTION** Just once in a while, rather than planning a detailed itinerary, it is nice to go for a wander, with no particular aim or theme in view, simply setting out to ride across country and waiting to see what happens. Quite often what happens is delightful. By no means all the pretty places of France are featured in the guidebooks, and I have often found the most memorable places on my travels are well off the beaten track and located quite by accident.

I found this route by simply heading east from Albi into the hills and valleys of the Rouergue, deciding to get back there in ten days or so. In the interval I would wander where fancy took me, turning up or down any road that looked interesting.

The terrain is very varied with plenty of hills, so one low gear will be helpful, and although there is accommodation available, much of the way lies through small villages, so a small tent might be useful. Thus equipped, take train and plane to the town of Albi on the Tarn where this tour begins.

\* \* \*

Albi is a very fine town, dominated by the great red-brick cathedral of Ste-Cécilia. This was the birthplace of the artist Toulouse-Lautrec and the museum in the Bishop's palace contains a vast collection of his work. It will probably take most

BOULOC

PONT DE SALERS

S

SALLES CURRAN

RODEZ

VILLEFRANCHE DE ROUERGUE

AMBIALET

NAJAC

ST. JUERY

LAGUÉPIE

ALBI

CORDES

ST. ANTONIN
NOBLE VAL

VAOUR

PENNE

GAILLAC

BRUNIQUEL

0

KILOMETRES

of the day to get to Albi, which is no bad place to spend a night, but leave early in the morning, heading up the south bank of the Tarn, through St-Juery (6km) and then on the minor D70, on a fine rolling ride to the village of Ambialet (35km), with splendid views over the river for most of the way.

Albi. The Cathedral dominates the town

Leaving Ambialet, and staying with the river as much as possible, head east all the way upstream to the little town of St-Rome-de-Tarn, some 70km away, allowing two days for this first section of the ride.

From St-Rome-de-Tarn I suggest going north, first up a long steep and winding ascent from the river valley, along which the views are outstanding. Then take the scenic route to Bouloc (17km). It took me three hours to ride to Bouloc, which gives some idea of the distractions, but then the café in the centre of Bouloc served an excellent inexpensive lunch which slowed me down still more! Ride on through gentle and descending countryside to Salles-Curan (9km) and the vast lake at Pareloup, a striking sight, virtually an inland sea in the middle of France, where a night stop and a swim will probably prove irresistible. From here ride north, through Pont-de-Salers (15km) on to the hilltop city of Rodez (21km). Rodez is worth a brief visit to see the cathedral, but then ride out, heading to the west, along the river Aveyron and stop for the night somewhere outside the town.

The Aveyron, which now gives its name to the former county

of Rouergue, is one of the lesser-known rivers of France, but is all the better for that. Follow it west, to the town of Villefranche-de-Rouergue (81km). Villefranche is a bastide, and as the name indicates, a French one, built by Alphonse de Poitiers (brother of St-Louis) in 1265. It is an interesting town, with a fine square, the Place Notre-Dame, and on the Albi road, just outside the town, the pilgrim church, La Chapelle des Étrangers, built for pilgrims on the Road to Compostela in 1451, is an example of the pure Gothic. From here turn south, down the gorges of the Aveyron past the great castle at Najac, built in 1253, to Languepie (49km). Here the Aveyron is joined by the river Viaur, and we continue to follow the river west, for it leads to some rare and little known places: St-Antonin-Noble-Val, the fantastical village of Penne, where the castle hangs out over the valley, and finally to pretty Bruniquel (55km) which also has a great medieval castle and is a very picturesque spot indeed, all narrow streets and leaning walls.

At Bruniquel ... decisions, decisions! An attractive scenic route leads south-west to Gaillac, where they have a very good white wine I had in mind to try, but a browse through a postcard rack settled the matter. I had to see the city of Cordes!

Set off east from Bruniquel on the D87 for Vaour (23km) and from there across country to the hilltop town of Cordes (24km), a splendid sight when seem from a distance, and no less attractive close to. Cordes is a medieval town built by Count Raymond VI of Toulouse in the middle of the thirteenth century. It became a centre for leather workers, *cordèliers*, hence the name, and it survived all the trials of the Hundred Years War and the Wars of Religion, but the population declined when the Wars were done, and the city had almost crumbled into ruin by the middle years of this century. Then artists and craftsmen discovered it and began to live there. They have gradually restored it to life, a very worthwhile task, and the town now lives again, beautiful and quite unspoiled. From Cordes it is a short 24km south to Caillac, for that good lunch and a bottle of that sparkling *Perle*, then the train for Toulouse and so home.

\* \* \*

As trips go this is a fairly short tour covering around 550km, but it is not the sort of journey one can rush. Many of the little towns and villages are set on hilltops and getting up there can add both time and distance to the day, though the chief distraction is the scenery. Roads which follow river valleys are by no means always flat and on this wandering journey I took the country as it came, riding fast when I felt like it or when the terrain permitted, walking up the longer hills, like the one from St-Rome-de-Tarn, and stopping frequently, which is the best way to enjoy this country, on a splendid and memorable tour.

MONTE CARLO
EZE
CAP FERRAT
VILLEFRANCHE
NICE
ANNOT
ST. PAUL DE VENCE
CAGNES
TAULANE
GRASSE
JUAN LES PINS
ANTIBES
CASTELANNE
CANNES
PONT SUBLIME
MOUSTIERS
FREJUS
ST. CROIX
MONT NEYAN
ST. MAXIME
ST. TROPEZ
PORT GRIMAUD
TAVERNES
ESPANNON
RIANS
ILE DU LEVANT
PIERREFEU DU VAR
POYLOUBIER
PORT CROS
HYÈRES
PORQUEROLLES
AIX EN PROVENCE
TOULON
GARDANNE
MIMET
GIENS
LA BOURDONNIERE
CROIX ROUGE
CASSIS
BANDOL
SANARY
MARSEILLE
LA CIOTAT

0    10   20   30   40   50   60   70   80   90
KILOMETRES

# TOUR 14
## The Côte d'Azur

**'Of all the pleasures in the world, travel is the most delightful.'**
**_Thomas Corgate_**, _Crudities_

---

| | |
|---|---|
| Distance: | 650km (405 miles). |
| Province: | Provence (Alpes-Maritimes). |
| Maps: | I.G.N. Carte Touristique No. 115 Provence Côte d'Azur. Michelin Regional 1:200,000 Nos. 245, 93, 81, 84. |
| Guidebooks: | Archibald Lyall, _Companion Guide to the South of France_, (Collins/Fontana). |
| Getting there: | By air, to Nice or Marseille. By rail, via Paris, to Nice or Marseille. |
| Time required: | Two to three weeks. |

**INTRODUCTION** It is fair to say that the English created the Côte d'Azur. It became the winter refuge for the rich and famous, an escape from their dreary northern winters, and until the 1930s no one dreamed of visiting this coast in summer. From April until October the Riviera was dead.

All that has changed and my first piece of advice regarding this tour is that the cyclist should, if possible, avoid this region in the high summer months of July and August. In those months the resort towns are crowded, the roads jammed with traffic and therefore quite dangerous, accommodation is difficult to find, and the weather is far too hot for comfortable touring.

As a glance at the I.G.N. 115 will quickly reveal, this is a mountainous coastline and, with the occasional plateau, the same applies to the hinterland, so one low gear of 30in or less will be very useful.

This tour will take two weeks and three would be even better. If possible save time by flying to Nice or Marseille, which you can do by scheduled airlines. Cheap fares are available and the time saving is considerable. This tour is described as from Marseille, but the link from Nice or the return to Marseille if the trip has to be short is easily made by rail, using a No. 40 _vélo en baggage à main_ connection. Rail links are quite good all over the Côte d'Azur, and one little train that could come in handy is the one which runs up into the hills from Nice to Digne, the Chemin-de-Fer-de-Provence.

As always, this tour uses minor roads whenever possible, and visits out of the way places as well as the better-known resorts. Where main roads must be used, and this is sometimes inevitable, I recommend riding either early in the day or between the hours of 1200 and 1400 when most French drivers will be safely tucked away in a restaurant.

\* \* \*

Arriving in Marseille, take half a day to explore the town. Make a boat trip round the interesting harbour where the Château d'If was the prison of the Count of Monte Cristo. From Marseille, ride out to the north and then east on the minor D8*bis*, through Croix Rouge to La Bourdonnière and turn north over the Pilon du Roi (670m) to Mimet, then on to Gardanne (12km). From there follow minor roads to Aix-en-Provence (7km). This makes a good first day's run, with a small mountain in the way to add a little spice. Aix is a university town with a fine art gallery. This is the country of Cézanne and Van Gogh, so take notice of the views, which may be familiar from their paintings.

Leave Aix for a tour of the 'arrière-pays', the back-country, heading east, past the peak of Mont-Ste-Victoire, to the castle of Puyloubier, and from there across open country to Rians (30km). Turn sharply east here, through Espannon to Tavernes (25km) and then turn north, cutting a corner off the main road to Mont Meyan, and down, on a minor road, the D71, to the great reservoir and lake at St-Croix (36km).

Circle the lake and head up to Moustiers (15km) at the start of the Gorges or Canyon du Verdon, one of the great natural wonders of France. It is possible to descend into the Canyon and walk through the depths of the Gorge, a two-day trip for fit, well-equipped walkers, but our route follows the southern rim, then up to the Pont Sublime and so to the town of Castellane (45km). Those in a hurry to reach the coast could pick up the Chemin-de-Fer-du-Provence by riding up to Annot (25km), but the tour continues by leaving Castellane, descending the N85, called the Route Napoléon, as quickly as possible, to the castle at Taulane, where the minor D-road leads off to the east, a wonderful route, all the way down to one of the gems of the Côte d'Azur, the little town of St-Paul-de-Vence (70km), a good day's run. At St-Paul be sure to see the paintings in the Hôtel de Colombe d'Or, explore the town and visit the art collection at the Fondation Maeght, before riding down to the coast at Cagnes and turning along the way into Nice.

Nice is a large city, full of hotels, with lots to see and do, and several excellent art galleries and museums. My advice is to leave the bikes here and spare a day or two to make trips along the coast or into the hills by train or coach, visiting Monte Carlo, Éze, or Grasse, using the bikes in the evenings, when riding out to Villefranche or Cap-Ferrat for dinner. After a day or two of this, you will want to get into the saddle again and

The hillside village of Entrevaux

head out west on the coast road. Follow the sweep of the Baie des Anges to Antibes, Juan-les-Pins, and Cannes, (30km). At Cannes, leave the coast and ride over the Estérel hills past Mont Vinaigre, to Fréjus, (36km). Fréjus, like many of these towns, was established by the Romans, for this is Provence remember, the 'Provincia Romana'.

At Fréjus, pick up the coastal road again and ride past St-Maxime, to Port Grimaud, a little version of Venice, and so into St-Tropez (35km). An evening by the *quai* in St Tro' to watch the crowds can be entertaining. Leave St-Tropez heading inland, then turn west after 12km on the very minor D14, winding directly west to the Pierrefeu du Var (38km) and there turn south for Hyères and little Giens, out on its isthmus, (35km). Take time out here for the boat trips along the coast to the Iles d'Hyères, to Porquerolles, and the Ile du Levant.

West of Giens, past the great naval base at Toulon, lie a string of attractive little resorts: Sanary, which is little-known and very pleasant; Bandol; La Ciotat; and Cassis (60km). The roads are busy but the faster cars and the heavier lorries usually stick to the nearby *autoroute*.

From Cassis ride north for 12km to Aubagne, the present home of the French Foreign Legion, which has a fascinating museum, or take boat trips along the coast to the lovely little bays or *calanques*, which indent the cliffs from here west to the Cap Croisette.

From here it is only a short ride into Marseille (25km) for the journey back to Britain.

\* \* \*

Although the Côte d'Azur is probably the most developed tourist area in Europe, it should not be seen simply as the last refuge of the hedonist. The scenery is outstanding, there are fine art galleries with unique collections, the towns contain excellent restaurants and the hinterland, behind the coast, is full of interesting places and empty of people. This tour will give the traveller a good sample of a most attractive region and show something of the great variety it has to offer.

The governing factors when planning a Côte d'Azur tour are the distance from the U.K., which really dictates air travel—certainly for a two-week stay—and the heavy traffic along the coast. The cyclist has to avoid this as much as possible by using minor roads but, alas, there are very few suitable minor roads along much of the coast, so diverting to bus, boat or train to see the more popular tourist centres is highly advisable, at least in summer.

If you like the area on this first acquaintance, why not come again, in a different season?

# TOUR 15
# A Tour of the Vendée

**'One of the pleasantest things in the world is going on a journey.'**
**William Hazlitt,** *On Going on a Journey*

---

| | |
|---|---|
| Distance: | 764km (475 miles). |
| Provinces: | Western Loire (Pays de la Loire), Poitou-Charentes. |
| Maps: | I.G.N. Carte Touristique No. 107 Poitou-Charantes. Michelin Regional 1:200,000 No. 232 Pays de la Loire and No. 233 Poitou-Charentes. |
| Guidebooks: | Michelin Green Guide, Côte de L'Atlantique. |
| Getting there: | Ferry to Roscoff or St-Malo, then via rail to Nantes. |
| Time required: | Two to three weeks. |

**INTRODUCTION** To be sure of good weather in France, you ought to go somewhere south of the Loire. Here lies the heartland of the country, which is inimitably French, and quite different in atmosphere from those areas more often visited by tourists. Too many cycletourists restrict their travels to the coastal provinces of Normandy and Brittany, and thereby miss a great deal of the ambiance of France, which is at its strongest only in places where most tourists don't go. It is, in fact, very noticeable that the numbers of cyclists decline south of the Loire, a situation which this book aims to correct. Even if time *is* short, judicious planning and the use of the night ferry and trains can take the traveller into the further parts of France without undue difficulty, and to this end, consider the country just south of Brittany, between the Atlantic coast and the county of Poitou, the Vendée, a pleasant corner, and one within easy reach.

The Vendée is a remarkable region with a beautiful coastline, and many fine offshore islands. Gifted with pretty ports, fine castles and some notable Romanesque churches, the coast is highly photogenic, while inland, apart from rolling countryside, lie the great drained marshlands, the *marais*, country which is quite apart from the noise and bustle of urban life.

NOIRMOUTIER

PORNIC

**NANTES**

LOIRE

KILOMETRES
0   10   20   30   40   50

FROMENTINE

NOTRE DAME DE MONTS

CLISSON

ST. GILLES

BEAUMARCHAIS
LA CHAIZE GIRAUD

CHAMBRETAUD

N

LES SABLES D'OLONNE

POUZAUGES LE VIEUX

LA CHÂTAIGNERAIE

GRUES   TRIAZE

PUY DE SERRE

LA FAUTE SUR MER

PUYRAVAULT

COULONGES

ILE DE RÉ

**LA ROCHELLE**

ILE DE OLERON

NIORT

ST PIERRE D'OLERON

ROCHFORT

BROUAGE

MARENNES

ST. JEAN D'ANGELY

ST JUST LUZAC

This tour begins in the Breton city of Nantes, a fine place and even if recently excised from the ancient province and placed in that artificial creation, the Pays de la Loire, it remains a distinctly Breton city. Getting there from the coast from St Malo or Roscoff will take two days on the road, so take the train, one of those coded 40 *Vélo en baggage á main*, via Rennes and save at least a day, remembering to note the times of code 40 trains from Nantes back to the coast for use on the return journey.

*   *   *

Nantes is a city which repays inspection, and is worth exploring. The great castle of the dukes of Brittany is just one essential sight. From there, ride across the Loire into the suburb of Réze, and then directly west on minor roads whenever possible, parallel to the busy main road, to the resort of Pornic (54km). As is usual close to any coast, minor roads are few, but after an evening in Pornic, a very pretty fishing port, ride south, around the bay of Bourgneuf, and then out to the west for a visit to the island of Noirmoutier, a fascinating place (56km) before turning south again to Fromentine (10km). Continue round the coast to the little town of Notre-Dame-de-Monts, and so down past St-Gilles for 50km to the minor road D12 which leads past the castle at Beaumarchais to La Chaize Giraud, and then on, south on the D32 to the great beaches of Les Sables-d'Olonne (25km).

Drift south from here to La Fauté-sur-Mer, a small resort (63km), choosing the coast roads with care for tidal inlets force many diversions inland on to main roads. This coastline is an attractive mixture of cliff and sandy beach, backed by forests, and as the journey takes us south the marshlands of the Parc Natural Regional du Marais Poitevin begin to open up to the east. This is often referred to as the *Venise Verte*, the Green Venice, an apt name for this region of lush grassland and canals. Cut into the *Venise Verte* through Grues and Triaize and go east to Puyravault (39km), before turning south still on minor roads for the attractive and historic seaport of La Rochelle (31km). On the way it is possible to stop and take a trip into the *marais* in large punts, but those who have not taken this opportunity should not miss the chance to take a ferry trip, to the offshore island of Ré. The Ile de Ré is 30km long from end to end, but the fortress at St-Martin-de-Ré and the lighthouse, the Phare de Balines, are just two reasons for visiting this island. Allow a day for the Ile de Ré, and spend at least an evening in La Rochelle before making a swift descent to yet another pretty port, the resort of Rochfort (32km). Rochfort is one of those dreamy little towns, with excellent inexpensive restaurants, and after a visit here, ride out on minor roads south across the marshes to the curious fortified town of Brouage. I consider Brouage to be one of the great and little-known gems of France, so don't miss it. From there go south and west to Marennes (7.5km), for our last island, the Ile d'Oléron (8km). A ride around this island will cover about 40km, before we

Ile de Oléron

leave the coastline and head back to the north on an inland route across the county.

Heading from St-Pierre-d'Oléron to St-Just-Luzac (27km), pick up the minor road, the D18, which runs north-east to St-Jean-d'Angely (53km). From here another minor road, the D120, leads directly north across the *marais*, skirting the town of Niort to the east all the way up to the little village of Coulonges, a marvellous ride of 68km.

At Coulonges take the D67 to Puy-de-Serre and continue on the D19 through La Châtaigneraie (27km) to Pouzauges-la-Vieux (20km). This lies in the hills of the Collines Vendéennes, which are not very high at around 288m, but make a contrast to the *marais*. From Pouzauges a scenic route, D752, leads north to Chambretaud (19km), then continue on minor roads to Clisson (39km), which has a fine castle. From here to Nantes the road leads across the wine country of Muscadet, and a bottle or two of that will be no great extra load in the panniers on the last 30km back to the starting point at Nantes.

*  *  *

A cycle trip through the Vendée and Poitou offers the traveller a most enjoyable and varied ride over moderate terrain with only the winds to worry about. As it happens they usually blow from the west and this can be helpful. There is a lot to see on this ride, fine golden Romanesque churches, little towns, fishing ports, small islands, remote and empty marshlands . . . delightful!

If you use the trains, all this is well within reach. The ridden distance is under 800km (depending on the island rides and various diversions) so that at the daily average of 80km this tour can be comfortably accomplished within two weeks, although three would be even better.

# TOUR 16
# A Tour of Languedoc-Roussillon

**'Fierce wars and love shall moralize my song.'**    ***Spenser,*** *Fairie Queene*

---

| | |
|---|---|
| Distance: | 750km (465 miles). |
| Provinces: | Languedoc-Roussillon, Midi-Pyrénées. |
| Maps: | I.G.N. Carte Touristique No. 114 Pyrénées-Languedoc. Michelin 1:200,000 Nos. 240 Languedoc-Roussillon and 235. |
| Guidebooks: | Neil Lands, *Languedoc-Roussillon*, (Spurbooks). |
| | Johnathan Sumption, *The Albigensian Crusade*, (Faber). |
| | George Savage, *The Languedoc*, (Barrie & Jenkins). |
| | Freda White, *West of the Rhône*, (Faber). |
| Getting there: | By air to Toulouse. |
| | By rail to Toulouse via Paris. |
| Time required: | Two to three weeks. |

**INTRODUCTION** This long and varied tour covers two linked but very different parts of France, the ancient country of Toulouse, which is all that is left of the old romantic Languedoc, and Roussillon, home of the French Catalans. This is Occitania, the Land of Oc, or it would be if the local separatist movements had their way. Once upon a time there were two languages in France. In the north the word 'yes' was 'oui' or 'ouil', but in the south it was 'oc' ... and so we get *Langue d'Oc*, but the differences between the two regions are more far-reaching. It is a colourful land, dominated by sea and mountain, with some splendid old cities, and many delightful out-of-the-way places, some of which we shall visit on this tour.

The history of the Languedoc is rather a sad one. The troubadour culture which evolved here, with songs, poetry and courtly love in the early Middle Ages, was quite extinguished in the bloody wars of the Albigensian Crusade, which the French kings used to destroy the counts of Toulouse and extirpated the religious sect of the Cathars. Even today, the Languedoc has still not recovered from those jarring days. Roussillon came to France late, in 1659, when Louis XIII and Richelieu pushed the Spanish back across the Pyrénées, and it remains a sharply Catalan country, even after 300 years.

The Languedoc lies far to the south, occupying much of the land from the southern edge of the Massif Central down to the Mediterranean and from the Rhône delta west to the Pyrénées. It will not be possible to cover all of it on one tour, so on this visit to the Languedoc we will see only a selection of what this region has to offer.

The journey begins in Toulouse, and although rail connections via Paris are excellent, to save time I recommend air travel if possible. The history of the area is both rich and complex, so reading one or more of the books listed above will add greatly to the traveller's enjoyment and appreciation of the trip, which begins in the old capital of the Languedoc, the red city of Toulouse.

\*   \*   \*

Toulouse is a big city, the fourth largest in France, and one well worth exploring. One essential visit is to the church of St-Sernin, a huge building now being restored, while an evening in the graceful Place de Capitoule is always entertaining.

Leaving Toulouse for the south-east, and preferably early in the morning before the traffic builds up, take the road through Castanet-Tolosan, until just past Montguiscard, where a minor road leads off onto the D16, on which the tourist can travel east to Castelnaudary (63km).

The towpath of the Canal du Midi can also be used for sections of this journey, for although the signs say that no wheeled vehicles are permitted, no one seems to object to cycles. Castelnaudary is a main port of the Canal du Midi, a great waterway built in the seventeenth century by Paul Riquet of Béziers and, if you enjoy towpath-riding, it can be followed for much of the way south across the winding hills of the Languedoc. The main roads, although wide and well-metalled, are all too often traffic-crammed, so use the towpath or the minor road from Castelnaudary, the D33, through Bram, to the next stop, the medieval *cité* of Carcassonne (36km).

The first sight of walled and turreted Carcassonne is unforgettable. This is the finest and best preserved medieval fortress town in Europe, a marvellous sight and a necessary stop on this tour of southern France. Close to, once inside the curtain walls, it fades a little, for Carcassonne is inevitably a tourist trap, but one that cannot be missed. Allow half a day in Carcassonne, before riding out to the south, to Limoux (29km) where they make a delicious sparkling wine, the *Blanquette de Limoux*, and then on to Couiza, (15km). Couiza has a fine castle, but a more curious and even more sinister place is the little village of Rennes-le-Château, a few steep kilometres to the east. In the 1920s, this village was the parish and home of a most unusual priest, Berengar Saunière, who suddenly came into great and still unexplained wealth. With this he built the road which climbs up to his village, and decorated the church in the most bizarre fashion. He also entertained a most strange group of friends and his refusal to explain the source of his prosperity led to the circulation of weird stories. Some say that he found the lost treasure of the Knights Templar, others that he unearthed the lost hoard of those Cathars burned for their faith at Montségur. Rumours that his prosperity was due to his involvement in black magic eventually led to Saunière being unfrocked, but legends apart, little Rennes is a very strange and pretty place, and one worth visiting.

South of Couiza, just before Quillan (10km) a scenic road leads east to Notre-Dame-de-Laval (20km) and then on to St-Paul-de-Fénouillet (11km) in the beautiful sharp-edged Fénouilledes, foothills of the Pyrénées. Turn south again here, and ride across the mountains, which are just agreeably high, down to Ille-sur-Têt, then east again to the city of the Catalans, Perpignan (24km).

Perpignan is a busy place, with much to see, including the great Palace of the kings of Mallorca, who ruled and lived hereabouts in the fourteenth century. In the centre of the town lies the red-brick medieval Castillet and the Place de la Loge where, on most summer evenings, everyone rises to dance the *Sardane*, the great folk dance of Catalonia.

From here the route lies to the north and east around the shores of the Golfe de Lion, but unless the tourist is really keen on covering the entire distance on the bike, on roads which lead through new and not very interesting resorts, I would recommend turning to the train. Before leaving Perpignan though, take a day off and ride south on the coastal road via Canet to the gem-like little port of Collioure (32km). A refuge for artists like Picasso, Collioure has a huge Templar castle, a pink-roofed Roman lighthouse, and many good restaurants, notably *La Bodega*, which is one of my favourite haunts. That apart, Collioure is very beautiful and if you have come this far, it should not be missed.

The main reason for urging a spot of train travel upon you is the presence of heavy traffic and the absence of suitable minor roads. This part of France straddles the main trunk route to Spain and the Costa Brava, so the traffic is far too heavy for comfort. Ride out of Perpignan for a look at the high and mighty fortress at Salses and from there take the train to Béziers. This will be no hardship, for the views across the *étangs* are excellent. Keep at least one eye open for flocks of pink flamingoes which are common hereabouts, wading in the shallow *étangs*.

Béziers is a fine city, a wine centre and the rugby capital of France. It would make a good night stop. It was sacked and almost totally destroyed in the opening stages of the Albigensian Crusade. The entire population was massacred and only the great cathedral remains of the original city which owed allegiance to the Counts of Toulouse.

From Béziers take the main road out to the east, and turn off after 10 km for Portiranges (5km) and follow the minor road D312 for Vias and Agde (12km). After Agde take the coast road D112, which is full of traffic but mercifully flat all the way to the ancient and attractive port of Sète, (20km). Sète was built as the terminal seaport for the Canal du Midi, and like most ports is a fascinating place. Sea-going ships tie up along the *quais* which are fringed with good restaurants. This was the birthplace of the poet Paul Valéry and there is an art gallery named after him. If you are lucky you may see the water-jousting between local teams, each trying to tip their rivals into the murky waters of the harbour.

After Sète, ride on to Frontignan (7km) and avoid the traffic by taking the towpath across the *étang* to Maguelone, Palavas and Carnon (25km). This towpath appears on the map as just a channel across the shallow *étang*, but it is a proper canal with a rough but perfectly ridable towpath.

From little Carnon, ride into La Grande Motte (9km) on the D21e, the biggest and most striking of all the new resorts built along the Languedoc coast, and turn inland here on the D979 for another rare and interesting place, the walled town of Aigues-Mortes (16km), which was built in the thirteenth century by St Louis as his port for the Seventh Crusade. It has not grown since, and is still contained within the original curtain walls. It is said that the Black Death arrived in Europe on a ship which docked at Aigues-Mortes, the city of the Dead Waters. After a visit to this fascinating and historic town, turn west, brave the traffic for a brief while (for 41km) to reach Montpellier, a classic French provincial city, certainly one of the most attractive in France. Give yourself an evening in the Place de la Comédie, or a pleasant meal in one of the restaurants in the Quartier de l'Ancien Courrier. This is the last touch of urban living on this trip, for from now on we will leave the modern comforts of the flat coastal plain and take the road back to Toulouse, through the hilly back-country of Languedoc.

First pick up a minor road, the D5, and head south and west to Pézenas (60km), a small but delightful little seventeeth-century town, once the home of the playwright Molière. Still on minor roads head past Servian for Cazouls (25km) north-west of Béziers, and then turn north, up the valley of the river Orb, for the beautiful village of Roquebrun, (20km) and so into

The Espinouse Mountains

the mountains of the Espinouse. At Tarassac (10km) turn west and follow the road through Olargues, and on to St-Pons (24km) where our route turns north, into the wild country of the Parc Regional du Haut Languedoc, a hilly ride across some dramatic country to Sidobre and the town of Castres (68km).

From Castres, Toulouse is within easy reach and there are good train connections if time is pressing. If not, then drift gently west, across the golden country of the Toulousain, through Puylaurens, Aguts, Caraman and Lanta, all little-visited places on the more minor roads, the only roads worth following, and back at last to the place where it began, the rosy-red city of Toulouse (70km).

\* \* \*

Plotting this trip on a map, the traveller will quickly see that it is a long ride, although by using the train for part of the coastal route some of the mileage can be eliminated. The problems however are not distance or terrain but traffic and heat. This is the warm south, the blissful Hippocrene. I am writing up this tour directly after having completed the ride, and even now, before the summer is fully into its stride, I have still to recover from the battering traffic on the road between Aigues-Mortes and Montpellier . . . but then I have very little tolerance for traffic, and one can make most of this journey on the quieter roads. This is beautiful country but too hot for comfort in July and August.

I wanted to see a selection of what this region has to offer, and this aim has been accomplished. The country of the Languedoc and Roussillon is very beautiful and very historic, so if time permits, try and see even more of it. Go further north, beyond the Monts de Lacune to Albi, and back towards Toulouse along the valley of the Tarn, or, in the years to come, return again to the striking golden land of the Cathars and the Catalans.

# TOUR 17
# A Mountain Tour of the Auvergne
### 'The reward of a thing well done, is to have done it.'
### **Emerson,** Essays

---

| | |
|---|---|
| Distance: | 532km (330 miles). |
| Province: | Auvergne. |
| Maps: | I.G.N. Carte Touristique No. 111, Auvergne. Michelin Regional 1:200,000 No. 239 Auvergne-Limousin. |
| Guidebook: | Peter Graham, *Portrait of the Auvergne*, (Hale). |
| Getting there: | By air or by rail via Paris to Clermont-Ferrand. |
| Time required: | Two weeks. |

**INTRODUCTION** Any choice of delights can be difficult, but if I had to choose my favourite part of France, I would, without hesitation, choose the Auvergne. To decide exactly why I like it is much more difficult, more complex even, but in the end it probably comes down to the scenery. Other parts of France may have finer towns and better food but the scenery of the Auvergne is unsurpassed, varied, and in many places really dramatic. This is the perfect province for lovers of the outdoors, ideal for walking and cross-country skiing, good indications that it is also ideal for cycletouring, especially if the tourist likes to travel through the high country. The Auvergne contains the volcanic part of the Massif Central and is studded, around Clermont-Ferrand, with the extinct craters of an explosive era. This tour takes in the volcano country, and the high parts and peaks of the Auvergne, climbing to the Puy de Sancy and the Puy Mary in the Monts du Cantal among others, so low gears and strong legs, even at the start, will be very useful. The daily distance will average around 60km.

Snow lies late in this part of France, and the summers are hot so, if possible, make this tour in the spring, in April or May when the meadows are deep with flowers, or in September or

CLERMONT
FERRAND

PUY DE DOME

BEAUNE

COL DE MORENO

PUY DE LA VACHE

RANDANNE

MUROL

LE MONT DORE

PUY DE SANCY

LA TOUR AUVERGNE

CHÂTEAU
DE VAL

BORT LES ORGUES

RION ES MONTAGNES

THOMAS

PUY MARY

AURILLAC

ARPAJON

ST. GERMAIN L'HERM

LA CHAISE
DIEU

ALLIER

CHILHAC

ST. FLOUR

N

0   10   20   30   40   50   60   70

KILOMETRES

October when the autumn tints are starting to appear. The tour begins in the city of Clermont-Ferrand.

* * *

Clermont has some fine old buildings, and a huge dark cathedral, but today it is mainly an industrial town, the home of Michelin tyres. Leave, heading directly west on the D68, for the heights of the Puy de Dôme (13km). This stands at 1464m and therefore offers great views in all directions. This is a steep climb to start the tour, but it is worth the effort and more will follow. The mountains of the Dômes are volcanic and run for 30km or more north and south of this central Puy, from which the traveller can see the cones of scores of extinct volcanoes.

Descend from the top and turn west, until the junction with the D52, which we follow south, over the Col de Moreno, past little Beaune to the D52e and then west, past the Puy de la Vache to Randanne (20km). Turn east here for 2km to pick up the D5 and head south to Murol (18km) which has a lake, lac Chambon, and a medieval château-fort; there are many such castles in the Auvergne, another of the region's many attractions.

From here go west, to Le Mont-Dore, and climb the road to the Puy de Sancy (1885m) (25km). Then head south-west, through La Tour d'Auvergne, all skiing country in winter, and down to the famous Château de Val near Bort-les-Orgues (36km). The château-fort of Val is a splendid sight, standing on an island in the lake.

From Bort-les-Orgues, go south to Thomas, (3km) and then take the D3 to the south-east, a marvellous road through Rion-es-Montagnes, past many castles, back into the mountain country, all the way to the second highest peak of the Monts de Cantal, the Puy Mary (1787m) (60km). Allow a full day for this and aim to stay in one of the little villages close to the summit amid this marvellous mountain scenery. This is skiing country in winter with no lack of accommodation, and it can get cold even in summer at this altitude.

From the top descend on the *Route des Crêtes* all the way to Aurillac (45km), a fine old town where we turn east for Arpajon (4km) and then wander eastwards on very minor roads all the way across country to St-Flour (87km). Choose the most direct road, for it is a long up-and-down way across the grain of this country, but St-Flour, high on the hill, is a marvellous sight at the end of the day and a good place to spend the night.

From St-Flour take the main road east for 20km to the D601 and then turn north for Chilhac (19km) and across country, still on D roads, to La Chaise-Dieu (42km), a good place to stay.

La Chaise-Dieu has a vast and magnificent abbey with a

famous mural of the 'Danse Macabre', which should certainly be seen. From here our road lies north, off the too well-beaten track, past St-Germain-l'Herm, (21km) and all the way along the spine of the Monts du Livradois, back to our starting point at Clermont-Ferrand (70km), a long and lovely ride with which to end this first but surely not last visit to the beautiful country of the Auvergne.

Abbey of La Chaise-Dieu

This mountain tour, circling the south from Clermont, has only revealed a little of what the Auvergne can offer. Magnificent though that sample is, there is plenty more. This journey has not visited the Vélay country around Le Puy or many of the river valleys which seam the land. It has, however, taken in most of the high, wild country and the most splendid majestic parts of this rugged landscape. Those hard riders who enjoy such mountain tours are in for the time of their lives.

# TOUR 18
# The Trans-Pyrénéan Ride

**'Two voices are there; that of the sea, and that of the mountains.'**

***Wordsworth,*** *Thoughts of a Briton on the Subjugation of Switzerland*

---

| | |
|---|---|
| Distance: | 720km (450 miles) |
| Provinces: | Midi-Pyrénées, Languedoc-Roussillon. |
| Maps: | I.G.N. Carte Touristique Nos. 113, Pyrénées-Occidentales and 114 Pyrénées-Languedoc. Michelin Regional 1:200,000 Nos 234 and 235 and 240 Languedoc-Roussillon. |
| Guidebooks: | Neil Lands, *The French Pyrénées*, (Spurbooks). |
| Getting there: | By air via Toulouse or Bordeaux. By rail via Paris to Hendaye and home via Perpignan. |
| Time required: | Two to three weeks. |

**INTRODUCTION** This long mountain tour follows a great deal of the route taken by fit, hard riders attempting the *Raid Pyrénéan*, which crosses the Pyrénées from west to east on the high route over the cols, or passes, which are such a feature of this mountain range. There are 18 cols between the Atlantic and the Mediterranean, and many thousands of feet of ascent, and those aiming to obtain the medal and certificate of the *Raid Pyrénéan* have to complete the journey in 100 hours or less. Good luck to them.

This tour, though over much the same route, should be more leisurely, and at an average of 80km per day can be completed in two weeks *provided* the rider is tour-fit, lightly loaded and has a machine equipped with suitable low gears, for the ascents are steep and long. On the other hand, so are the descents.

The real attraction of this tour, apart from the challenge it presents to those who enjoy mountain touring, must lie in the spectacular and beautiful scenery, but a word of warning about the weather. I have seen snow blocking the Col du Tourmalet in early July, so this ride has to be made in high summer. Even

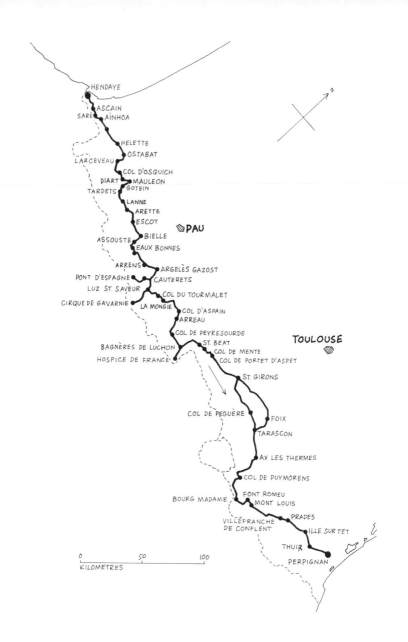

then it can be very cold on the tops and during the descents, so some warm and windproof clothing is always advisable.

Time being critical, air travel is recommended. A return air ticket via Toulouse will be cheaper than a split journey via Bordeaux and Perpignan, but the rail connections to the start of the tour at Hendaye are much easier from Bordeaux.

\* \* \*

From Hendaye, head east through three lovely Basque villages, Ascain, Sare, and Aïnhoa (53km) then north and east to Itxassou (16km) and then, on the D119, through Hélette and Ostabat to Larceveau (45km). The D918 from here climbs to the first col, the Col d'Osquich (392m) and then down past Ordiarp to the town of Mauléon-Licharre (24km). Turn south here to see the classic Basque church at Gotein and on up the valley to Tardets, then east to Lanna and Arette (39km), descending into the valley of the Aspe. Turn south here, weaving across the mountains to Escot, then east again, over the Col de Marie Blanque to Bielle in the valley of the Ossau (20km). This pattern of riding up and down the various river valleys to the start of a steep climb should be well established by now, and it will continue like this for the rest of the journey, and the highest cols are just about to put in an appearance.

At Bielle turn south for 10km to Assouste, and then up, through Eaux Bonnes and the ski resort of Gourette, over the high and very beautiful col d'Aubisque (1709m) and the col de Soular (1474m), down past Arrens to Argelès-Gazost (46km). The scenery and views on this section of the route are quite superb.

South of Argelès lie a couple of places which are well worth a visit, or even a day off to explore if time permits. First, above the spa town of Cauterets lies the Pont d'Espagne, an attractive region of the National Park of the Pyrénées. East of here, at the end of another main road, lies the great rock wall of the massive Cirque du Gavarnie (32km), one of the great natural wonders of the Pyrénées. This is a sight that every traveller will remember, the sheer rock face split by a long lace-like waterfall. The little town of Luz-St-Sauveur nearby, has a curious battlemented church and the road east from there leads up and up (and up) to the highest col of the route, the Col du Tourmalet (2115m), before descending, past the ski resort of La Mongie to the valley of Campan (35km). Turn south and then east again over the Col d'Aspin (1489m) to Arreau (26km) and then take another long, hard ride over the Col de Peyresourde (1569m) down to the spa town of Bagnères-de-Luchon.

The 400km (250 mile) long wall of the Pyrénées is not a continuous chain. There is a gap in it, just to the east of Luchon, the Val d'Aran, through which the river Garonne, called here the Garona, runs over into France. The Spanish frontier actually lies north of the watershed here, and one popular excursion from Luchon is the path up to the frontier at the Hospice de France, a must for walkers.

It is possible to cross over into Spain and ride north, back into France, thus bagging another col, the Col du Portillon (1293m) which marks the frontier, but otherwise turn north, towards St-Bertrand-de-Comminges, through St-Beat and over the Col de Mente (1349m) and the Col de Portet d'Aspet, on to the town of St-Girons.

St-Girons is a pleasant town on the main N117 road which skirts the foot of the French Pyrénées and provides an escape route if exhaustion is now setting in, or you have had enough

The High Pyrénées

of these endless mountains. You can follow the N117 to Foix, a very interesting and historic town, and so rejoin the route at Tarascon (60km) or, if the legs are now strong, strike off south on the minor road up past the Col de Peguère (1375m), a long and winding road, and reach Tarascon after 58km.

At Tarascon turn south-east to another little spa town, Ax-les-Thermes (26km), and then on to the turn-off to the south, for the Col de Puymorens (1915m) (25km). From here the road climbs to the high plateau of the Cerdagne, arriving at last at the town of Bourg-Madame (30km). Then follows a pleasant and fairly flat ride across the high Cerdagne to Font Romeu and the fortress town of Mont Louis.

From here the end of the road is almost in sight. If time is very short the journey to Perpignan can be made in the little tourist train, *le petit train jaune*, which runs from the Cerdagne, a fine trip to the plains below. However, it is mostly downhill from now on and the descent to the wine-drenched plains of Roussillon is one of the most spectacular of the trip. From Villefranche-de-Conflent the road runs on down to the valley of the river Têt, to Prades, Ille-sur-Têt, past Thuir and the gem-like little town of Castelnau and so to Perpignan, capital of French Catalonia.

From here there are good rail connections and regular flights to the U.K. with the blue waters of the Mediterranean just a few kilometres away, a fair reward at the end of a long, hard journey.

\* \* \*

On this trip the traveller has spanned the Pyrénées from the land of the Basques to the country of the Catalans, and toured a part of France where few visitors ever go. It is a long way and, since this is not a journey which anyone is likely to make twice, my advice is to allow three weeks for the journey and make the most of it. If there are indeed two voices, that of the sea, and that of the mountains, the traveller on this tour can hear them both.

LE PUY
CORDES
BAINS
MONISTROL
SAUGUES
ST. CHELY D'APCHER
AUMONT
AUBRAC
NASBINALS
AUBRAC
ESTAING
ST. CÔME
CONQUES
ESPALION
VILLECOMTAL
DECAZEVILLE
FIGEAC
MARCILHAC
CABREKETS
CAHORS
LAUZERTE
MOISSAC
ST. NICOLAS
DE LA GRAVE
LAVIT
MARSAC
LECTOURE
TOULOUSE
CONDOM
EAUZE
AIRE SUR L'ADOUR
GEAUNE
HAGETMAU
TARBES
ORTHEZ
PAU
SALIES DE BEARN
SAUVETERRE DE BEARN
ST. PALAIS
OSTABAT
ST. JEAN DE
PIED PORT

GARONNE

0     50     100     150
KILOMETRES

N

# TOUR 19
# The Road to Compostela
# Le Puy to the Pyrénées

**'Then Palmers long to seeke the stranger
strands,
Of far-off saynts hallow'd in divers lands.'**
***Chaucer,*** *The Canterbury Tales*

---

| | |
|---|---|
| Distance: | 620km (375 miles). |
| Provinces: | Auvergne, Midi-Pyrénées, Pyrénées-Occidentales. |
| Maps: | I.G.N. Carte Touristique, Nos. III, Auvergne and 113, Pyrénées-Occidentales. Michelin Regional 1:200,000 No. 239 Auvergne Limousin, No. 235 Midi-Pyrénées. |
| Guidebooks | Walter Starkie, *The Road to Santiago*, (John Murray). |
| | Edwin Mullins, *The Pilgrimage to Santiago*, (Secker & Warburg). |
| Getting there: | By air to Le Puy via Lyon (Satolas) and then by train. |
| | By rail via Paris and Clermont-Ferrand. |
| | Home: By the rail link from St-Jean-Pied-de-Port to Bayonne, Bordeaux and Paris. |
| Time required: | Two to three weeks. |

**INTRODUCTION** I have always believed that most kinds of travel are improved if the trip has a reason, a theme or an objective. In my particular case, if the trip has plenty of history, so much the better, and no journey in Europe is so evocative of the past as the old pilgrim road which leads across France to the shrine of St James at Santiago de Compostela in Spanish Galicia. This journey covers one of the French roads, down to the Spanish frontier. Pilgrims have been making their way to Santiago de Compostela for at least a thousand years and the pilgrimage still continues today, although I suspect that love of travel and history motivates more travellers on the Road than strong religious feelings. Whatever the personal motivation though, as the Feast of St James (Santiago), 25 July, approaches, the road to Santiago comes alive again and every year hundreds of travellers make this journey, many of them on cycles. The route is clearly marked and not a lot has changed over the last thousand years, so that this journey is a piece of living history, as valid today as it ever was, and the perfect tour.

This trip is a story as well as a journey, and the traveller will enjoy the trip far more if he or she first reads one of the books listed above, which tell, in some detail, the legends and past of this historic pilgrimage. The story continues, and those who take the 'cockleshell', the symbol of St James, are becoming a part of history, a pleasing thought.

On a more mundane level, the Road is long and the summers are usually hot, so the minimum of kit and at least one low gear will be useful. A scallopshell (the *coquille de St-Jacques*), tied to the front of the bike-bag, will identify the traveller as a Compostela pilgrim, and this can be most useful, for help is always forthcoming to travellers on the Road. There are, in fact, four historic roads, from Paris, Le Puy, Arles, and Vézelay. I have chosen to follow the one from Le Puy, which is not the easiest route but it is the one I know best and it takes in some of the most picturesque and impressive places.

*   *   *

Arriving at Le Puy, take a little time to look around this city which is unusual and striking; visit the cathedral and the little pilgrim chapel on a needle-spike of rock, which overlooks the city, before heading west on the D589 to Cordes, Bains and Monistrol by the deep gorges of the river Allier (30km) and so to Saugues (15km). From here the Road crosses the mountains of the Margaride, which peak at around 1400m and then rises and falls to the town of St-Chély-d'Apcher (41km). From here go south on a stretch of main road N9 to Aumont-Aubrac, (10km) and there turn west on the D987 for Nasbinals. The Road now crosses the high, windy plateau of the Aubrac, a glorious little-known place, a paradise in the late spring when the flowers are out. In the centre of this plateau lies the village of Aubrac, built in the Middle Ages to shelter Compostela pilgrims. The present *gîte d'étape* is in the old *donjon* of the castle which once stood there, the Tour des Anglais. Little Aubrac is a lovely spot, and from here the Road falls away, on a long, long descent down into the valley of the Lot, at St-Côme (27km).

Turn down the river valley through two fine towns, Espalion and then Estaing (13km) which has a magnificent castle. At Estaing turn west on the D22, and follow this road to the valley of the Dourdou, through Villecomtal, and up to the town of Conques (40km). Conques is one of the most beautiful little towns in France, and an essential stop on the pilgrim Road, with a huge cathedral which contains the relics of yet another saint, Ste Foy. Take time to explore Conques and be sure to see the reliquary of Ste Foy in the Cathedral treasury. Allow a full day to see Conques and stay the night.

From Conques, take the minor road west, past the chapel of St-Roch and the Croix du Pargadou, a stiff climb and on to Decazeville, (15km). From here take the main N-road to Figeac (28km), a pleasant riverside town, much more attractive than Decazeville.

Leaving Figeac, follow the main D13 for 6km before turning off on the D41, for the valley of the river Celé, through Marcillac, another pilgrim stop, and through Cabrerets, to the town of Cahors, (70km) where the river Lot is spanned by that famous and picturesque fortified bridge, the Pont Valentré.

A little south of Cahors, the D653 leads off to the right, and 1km after the turn the D7 heads for the south to Lauzerte (30km) and a night stop at the town of Moissac (22km). The cloisters and the tympanum of the cathedral at Moissac are two more works of art on the pilgrim Road and have to be seen.

Leave Moissac for the west and cross the river for St Nicolas-de-la-Grave, and then follow the Road south and west, on minor roads, for Lavit, Marsac and Lectoure (40km). This is the country of the Gers, a hilly, rippling land and the Road leads on, following a scenic route to Condom (21km), and then, on a main road, to Eauze (29km) and Aire-sur-l'Adour (36km).

At Aire, take the cross-country roads for Geaune and Hagetmau (34km) where the Road turns south for Orthez, another ancient place with a fortified bridge, and so west and south to Salies-de-Béarn, Sauveterre-de-Béarn, and on to the next major stop on the Road, at St-Palais, in the Basque country of Navarre, (40km). On a hill with the curious name of Gibraltar, just above St-Palais, an obelisk marks the spot where three of the French routes come together for the crossing of the Pyrénées. It is a steep climb up to Gibraltar, but well worth it. Compostela road signs, marking places of interest on the pilgrim Road, now appear with increasing frequency, and they will lead the traveller to Ostabat and the little chapel at Harambels, while reeling off the last 30km of Road to the end of the French section of this historic journey, in the frontier town of St-Jean-Pied-de-Port.

\* \*. \*

This tour is a journey for those who love history, and to my mind the finest traveller's road left in Europe. From St-Jean the Road leads on, across the Pyrénées by the pass of Ronces-valles, where Roland fell, to Pamplona of the Basques, the plains of Navarra and the *meséta* of Castile, over the green mountains of Galicia to the good city of the Apostle. But that is another country and another story.

Conques

# TOUR 20
# The End-to-End: St-Malo to Sète

**'The great object of travel is to see the shores of the Mediterranean.'** *Dr Johnson*

---

| | |
|---|---|
| Distance: | 1124km (700 miles) |
| Provinces: | Brittany, Pays de la Loire, Poitou, Limousin, Midi-Pyrénées, Languedoc-Roussillon. |
| Maps: | For planning: Michelin Red, 1cm:10km. En route: Michelin Regional maps 1:200,000 (1cm:2km); |
| | Nos. 230 Bretagne |
| | 232 Pays de la Loire . |
| | 233 Poitou-Charentes |
| | 235 Midi-Pyrénées |
| | 240 Languedoc-Roussillon. |
| Guidebooks: | Many available on each of the above regions (see list in bibliography). Tom Vernon's *Fat Man on a Bicycle* (Fontana) is the perfect tale of such a journey, an inspirational work. |
| Ports: (out) | Portsmouth to St-Malo (Brittany Ferries) |
| (home) | By air—Palma Mallorca to Gatwick (Air Europe). |
| Time required: | Ten days. |

**INTRODUCTION** This tour does not follow the pattern of those which precede it, for the motivation was different. The other tours are designed to offer attractive and varied holiday journeys through different parts of France. This one is more of a test, an adventure, or, if you will, a challenge. For the record, I am not very interested in self-inflicted challenges; life is difficult enough. However, there were other compelling motivations. How else or how better to end a book on cycletouring in France than with a journey across country from the Channel to the Mediterranean? Wise men will always listen to the dictates of Dr Johnson. Then, as journeys go, it interested me because I had never done it before and if the advice and information in this book was to be current and relevant, surely I should

ST. MALO

COMBOURG
MARCILLE RAOUL

VITRE
ARGENTRÉ DU PLESSIS
CRAON
SÉGRÉ

*SARTHE*

*LOIR*

*LOIRE*
ANGERS
BRISSAC

*VIENNE*

POITIERS
GENÇAY
ST. SECONDIN

CONFOLENS

CHALUS

SEGUR LA CHÂTEAU

*ISLE*
BRIVE
*DORDOGNE*

ROCAMADOUR
GRAMAT
*LOT*
FIGEAC
CAPDENAC GARE

RODEZ
*AVEYRON*
PONT DE SALARS
BOULOC
*TARN*
L'HOSPITALET
LA COUVERTOIRADE
LE CAYLAR
ST. PIERRE DE LA FAGE
MONTPEYROUX
MONTARNAUD
ANIANE
SÈTE
PALAVAS
LES FLOTS

N

0  20  40  60  80  100  120  140  160  180  200
KILOMETRES

bike off on a more or less unplanned trip and see what happened, writing it up on a day-by-day basis as an example of what actually occurs on a typical cycletour.

Finally, I think that every cycletourist one day will want to see the shores of the Mediterranean, and since my next cycletouring book will be set in Spain, why not end this one with my arrival in that country?

There were also, of course, constraints. The chief controlling factor was time. I had work enough to keep me over-occupied until the end of July and in fact posted off the last article to a newspaper 15 minutes before leaving for the start of this journey. I had also promised family and friends that I would join them in Mallorca for our family holiday by the middle of August, and with only two ferries a week from Sète, my chosen port for Palma, this too limited my time. I would need to ride at least 100km a day, the month was August and the weather was hot. Being busy I had had no time to train or get tour-fit. Oh well!

**Route** It was necessary to decide on a route early because the ferries were bound to be crowded. I opted for the Brittany Ferry route from Portsmouth to St-Malo, partly because it offered a considerable lift on the road south, partly because an overnight sailing would give me a good night's sleep and an early start. It also offered the shortest end-to-end route and I was not averse to that either. The local British Rail Information Office told me that there was no reason why one of two trains should not transport bike and self to Portsmouth by a respectable hour, so getting to France seemed feasible, and the ferry from Sète to Palma was booked through a friend in Paris.

Getting home again was more problematic, for it was still peak holiday time. Flights were crowded, and nasty, knobbly cycles were unwelcome in the luggage holds. I had no wish to be parted from my precious steed, and eventually discovered that Air Europe will carry cycles as a matter of course and had space on their flights from Palma. That took care of the parts at either end, but what of the bit in the middle?

**KIT** On kit, the rule is simple: the less the better. Carry clothing on the one-on, one-off, and one-in-the-wash principle. Given warm weather I can wash each day's clothing that evening which, apart from supplying what the Americans coyly describe as 'personal freshness', means that fewer clothes are necessary. A bottle of shampoo serves equally for washing hair and clothes, and my kit list for this trip was as follows:

**To wear:**

1 T-shirt

1 neckerchief

1 pair Rohan shorts

1 pair underpants

1 pair socks

1 pair trainers

1 handkerchief

1 pair gloves

1 pair sunglasses

**Clothing carried:**

1 Rohan Pampas jacket

2 T-shirts

2 pairs underpants

2 pairs socks

1 pair shorts

1 pair cotton trousers

1 pair Rohan trousers

2 handkerchiefs

1 wind- and waterproof jacket

1 sun hat

**Toilet and medical:**

lip salve

sun cream

washing and shaving gear

first-aid kit (aspirin, plasters etc.)

bottle shampoo

towel

**Camping equipment:**

1 Robert Saunders Jet Packer tent

1 Blacks Icelandic sleeping bag

1 Thermarest self-inflating mattress

1 Trangia kettle and cook-pot

1 Camping Gaz Globe Trotter stove

2 spare cartridges

knife, fork, spoon

bottle opener

**Trip equipment:**

passport

tickets

money

U.K. chequebook

pens

1 Nikon FM2 SLR camera with 1 × 43–85mm zoom lens

1 Olympus 35mm RC camera

4 rolls (36) Kodak 64 film

4 rolls (36) Ilford 125 film

**Cycle tools and spares:**

2 spare inners

1 spare cover

6 spare spokes

1 set brake blocks

1 rear brake cable

1 rear gear cable

puncture repair outfit, spoke key,

pliers, screwdriver, multi-spanner,

Allen keys, security chain with combination lock, 2 shock-cords.

All the above went very comfortably into two Karrimor 'Iberian' panniers and a handlebar bag. Note that I took no traveller's cheques, food or maps. With a Eurocheque card most French banks will cash English cheques; food I prefer to purchase on a day-to-day basis; maps are cheaper in France and readily obtainable.

**PREPARATION** It is fair to say that the bike started the journey a good deal fitter than I did. I plead lack of time and would in self-defence justify this feeble answer by pointing out that freelance writers do not always have evenings to spare for cycle rides, but I can speak from current experience when I say that anyone intending to embark on a trip which will involve riding 100km a day or more, day after day, in hot weather, should regard some pre-departure rides to get fit as thoroughly advisable.

At least I had the cycle thoroughly serviced and replaced both tyres, with the resulting benefit of only one puncture. The gears were changed to those described on page 24, by swapping the front rings of my 52-42 Carlton Corsair, putting the 42-tooth on the outside and a 36-tooth ring on the inner. This, with the existing rear block, gave me a nice range of gears and a top of 81in, a little low on the flat but ideal for grinding up long, long hills with 14kg of kit and temperatures up around 90°F or even higher.

So, with the gear packed, the cycle ready and the rider out of condition, let us wave goodbye to our friends, now seen assembled and waving outside my home, and set off for France.

\* \* \*

**Day one—getting to France** The 20 miles or so to the main railway station from my home took a pleasing hour and a half. After a slight argument with the lady train guard who didn't like cycles (or me) the machine was shock-corded to the waggon wall and we trundled off to Guildford. Off here without trouble and the Portsmouth connection arrived within a few minutes. Again no problems and by just after eight o'clock I am riding towards the Portsmouth ferry terminal. 'Go to the front of the queue', says the checker-in, ripping my ticket, and a very smug feeling it is to sail past the fuming motorists up to the head of the line.

About 30 other cycletourists are already there. Karrimor panniers seem very popular and if most of the machines look very heavily laden that's not my problem. 'We try to cut down on the load every year,' said one family man, comparing his pile of kit with mine, 'but somehow it always creeps up again.'

Sailing time approaches, the cyclists are checked in first, we ride down to the car-deck and secure our machines to various stanchions along the bulkheads (or walls to those with no nautical connections). Lengths of rope are provided for this purpose, but my shock-cords come in handy and are much admired. The cycle tribe have dumped their panniers in their cabins and occupied the bar before the first motorist has even come on board. We sail on time, the cabin is comfortable and the sea is calm. When I come on deck at 07.30 hours next morning the ship is already weaving through the rocky approaches to St-Malo and by 08.30 hours we are ashore. My journey to the Mediterranean has at last begun.

**DAY TWO** It began, *pace* Tom Vernon, at a cafe inside the walls, the Intra-Muros of old St-Malo, drinking a coffee. I needed the *Maison de la Presse* to open because I needed a map. This purchased, the regional 1:200,000 Michelin to *Bretagne*, I had yet another coffee and began to plan the first of many route revisions, seeking ways to cut the distance and avoid main roads. This was Friday, the last Friday in July and the day of *Le Départ*, the start of the French holiday season, when every French family crams the car with luggage and sets off at high speed for the coast, hoping not to kill people on the way. The carnage and the crashes are often formidable, and main roads are therefore best avoided. I decided against the direct route to the Loire through Rennes and headed a little east of south, through Combourg and come down to the Loire at Angers, passing through Vitré. I left St-Malo at 09.15 and reached Combourg, once the home of the writer Chateaubriand, at 11.15 with 37km done and going well.

I took lunch in a *Routiers* cafe at Marcille-Raoul where four courses and half-a-litre of wine cost only 45 francs (£4). The wine was a mistake. I soon discovered that 'en vélo there is veritas' and that even two glasses of wine at lunchtime could cut my legs from under me on a hot afternoon. My advice is to avoid alcohol at lunchtime, for that afternoon became hard work, all the way to the magnificent walled city of Vitré, where I had tea and eventually, at 20.00 hours, I arrived at Argenti-ère-du-Plessis, 9km south of Vitré, having covered 115km that day. All the hotels were closed, which seemed crazy in the middle of the holiday season, and the small campsite looked decidedly mosquito-infested, but there was an excellent A.B.R.I. gîte d'étape, which with hot showers, (very essential after a day on the road) a bunk, and use of the well-fitted kitchen, cost only 19 francs. I cooked, ate, washed my clothes free from that day's sweat and road dust, and slept like a log.

**DAY THREE** In spite of various good resolutions, I got away late, after 09.00 hours, but dashed off a quick 29km to Craon, a pretty town, in one-and-a-half hours. I saw a woodpecker, wrens, lots of finches in the woods and, on the road to Seagré, met another couple of cycletourists, also heading for Sète. Mutual surprise! He was a professor of French from Southampton and, with his French wife, they were on their latest annual cycle tour of France. Over lunch they told me that most of the cycletourists they had met over the years had been British, but that the number usually dwindled rapidly south of the Loire. They also expressed doubts about the use of the regional railway network to get about the country and save time, but agreed that when transporting bikes about the main lines, French beaurocracy actually worked. 'We'll get back via Paris and put our bikes on the train at Sète a couple of days before we leave ourselves, picking them up, all numbered, at the Gare-de-Lyon, when we arrive later. We always have and there has never been any difficulty.'

By mid-afternoon, thirsty for tea, I arrived at Angers, a big city, swamped on that Saturday by the influx of *La Départ*. Here I got lost and coming up to some traffic lights caught my foot in the toe-clip and fell heavily into the road. Grazed, bleeding and more than a touch miffed, I was soothed by tea and crossed the river Mayenne and then the great Loire itself, the first major landmark in my journey (Hooray!). About 19.00 hours I arrived at Brissac, 25km south of Angers with another 115kms under my wheels, and getting quite tanned. Dinner in the Restaurant du Commerce cost only 45 francs for a great spread—and so to bed.

**DAY FOUR** Day four began with a problem. I had had my pump stolen on a previous tour and therefore purchased a new one, which I had not yet needed to use. However, the rear tyre seemed a little soft so I applied the pump and sssssssh . . . all the air rushed out. The pump connection was faulty. Here I was in a small village, with a flat tyre and a useless pump, on a Sunday morning! One must be resourceful. I removed the wheel, tramped up to the main highway and in a couple of minutes a French cyclist appeared. I demonstrated my plight, he inflated my tyre, we smiled, he left.

Day four looked up from then on, at least for a while. I raced out of Anjou into the country of Poitou, through the rose-encrusted Doué-la-Fontaine, and across the rolling countryside to the town of Poitiers, where had I any sense I would have stayed, with nearly 100km on the clock. It was, however, only 17.00 hours and I thought to ride out a little, not realising that *La Départ* tidal wave had now arrived in central France. All the hotels were full and the campsites conspicuous by their absence. Anyway, I couldn't find one and so rode on and on, in the gathering dark. I could have camped behind a hedge, but at the end of the day a cycletourist needs a bath or a shower, and the hope of one or the other kept me going. Presently, it began to rain.

At last, with 147km done that day, I found a small 'camping' in the village of St-Secondin, south of Gençay, put up my tent, made some coffee and crawled into my sleeping bag just as the heavens opened. An almighty storm, with lots of lightning, raged most of the night and I slept very little.

**DAY FIVE** Up betimes, or just after first light to be exact, and by 07.00 I was on the road and thankful to get away. This area of France had been ravaged by storms in recent weeks and in daylight the devastation was startling. Trees with shattered trunks lay everywhere and most of the roofs were covered with tarpaulins, as their slates had been ripped off. It rained again in the morning, giving me that by now overdue bath, but as I arrived at Confolens on the river Vienne, the sun came out. Lunch there in a cafe overlooking the river and at 16.30 with some 91km done that day, I arrived at Châlus, found a room in the Hôtel Carrefour, and decided enough was enough. A hot shower, wash all the clothes, then a stroll, ice-cream in hand, to the walls of the castle in front of which our King Richard Coeur-de-Lion met his death in 1199, then dinner, yet another shower, and with no great reluctance, to bed.

**DAY SIX** We are in the south now, one can see that. The roofs have red tiles, not grey slates, and the vineyards, which I have seen since Angers, continue to multiply.

After nine hours sleep I felt good. In fact I felt very good, fitter now and ready to roll. Breakfast and an interesting run to Brive, an exciting ride of 99 km with plenty of photo-stops along the way, notably at the beautiful village of Ségur-le-Château, one of those picture-postcard places.

Brive was busy, bustling in fact, full of cars and not the place for me. I wanted tranquility, but I didn't get it. The road south from Brive, the N20, is a main artery and a nightmare! The traffic in the late afternoon was nose to tail and the huge five-axle *camions* all too frequent. Any wise cyclist will beware of Belgians armed with caravans, and this was no fun at all.

To be fair, it was all my own fault. I had intended to leave Brive by the second-class D road and go south via Beynat and Beaulieu, but I didn't, with these dire results. At 17.30 I had had enough of dicing with death for one day, and when a big Relais Routiers hotel and cafe appeared on the right I swerved off through the traffic and stopped for the night. These Routier cafés and hotels, although designed for lorry drivers, are good places to stay. I had a hot shower, a drink at the bar and a pleasant evening with the hard-eating and hard-drinking truckers. I also arranged an 06.30 call with the intention of getting off the N20 as soon as possible, certainly before the traffic could build up, and with this in mind went early to bed.

**DAY SEVEN** Just for once my resolution held good. A quick coffee and I was on the road by just after 07.00 hours, racing down and off the main road for breakfast in the spectacular pilgrim town of Rocamadour, where the houses cling to the cliffs. Then on to Gramat, a quick drink of *Orangina* (the cyclist's staple) and a ham sandwich for lunch before pressing on to the attractive riverside town of Figeac. Figeac is, or was, the home of Champollion, who deciphered the secrets of the Rosetta Stone and so cracked the code of the Egyptian hieroglyphics. That apart, it's a pretty place.

From Figeac, in the late afternoon, I climbed the hill and then enjoyed a long swoop down to the little town of Capdenac Gare, to find a station and discover if trains in provincial France would be of any practical help to the wandering cyclist. The problem is simple: can a cyclist use provincial trains to skip about the country at the end of the day or avoid the boring bits, without being parted from his or her machine? According to the SNCF brochures there are over 2000 trains daily where cycles can be carried as hand baggage; here, in the very heart of France, seemed a good place to test the situation for, as you will have noted, I had heard differently. As I had already done 98km that day and crossed this region on a previous tour, I didn't feel too guilty about taking a train in the evening.

Relax, gentle cyclist, it all proved surprisingly easy. First, into the Information Office and pop the question. The lady consulted her *horaire*; the 16.07 train to Rodez carried the magic code number 40; *vélos en baggage à main*. I bought a ticket for 30 francs, the cycle travelling free. When the train arrived I put my cycle into the luggage van, and by 17.30 was cycling up the hill into the red city of Rodez.

There is clearly no need for any cyclist to restrict tours to regions north of the Loire or just within striking distance of the Channel ports. Use the trains to get about a bit, or as a help on the journey to the blissful south.

**DAY EIGHT** Up early at Rodez. First a visit to the bank which opened at 08.15 to cash an English cheque and then a minor road out to Pont-de-Salars and the beautiful lake at Pareloup, a marvellous spot with many campings, virtually an inland sea. This day's ride was among the most memorable of the entire journey, for the countryside was quite lovely, and the roads virtually empty.

In the little village of Bouloc, stopping to refill my water bottle from the village fountain, I heard some happy cries from the local café and had a long, cheap and splendid lunch, which went on seemingly for hours. A word here about water. In this

The Cathedral at Rodez

heat I was drinking water in large quantities, and there are two schools of thought about this practice. One says: never drink the water or only if it comes out of a bottle. The other says: drink the lot and damn the consequences. Outside the East I belong to the latter school, and so far have come to no harm by it. By now I must be immune to most bugs, but drifting across France the changes in the taste of the water from place to place were most noticeable. This, from the fountain in little Bouloc, was like nectar.

The afternoon ride was wonderful, descending the long road down to the green Tarn. This descent goes on for miles and I had to stop several times to let the rims cool as the brakes heated them and I was afraid that the tubes would explode. When I dripped a little water onto the rims they spat and steamed. So the day wore on, too long but always delightful until I clocked up another 120km on the road south, and climbed at last to the chilly heights of the Causse du Larzac, and found a campsite by l'Hospitalet, where I was offered dinner by a nice couple of cycletourists from Australia, and went to bed by starlight.

**DAY NINE** The night was cold. The high plateaux of the Causse country lie at the 1000m mark, so I was glad of my down-filled sleeping bag. By then I had learned—or rather re-learned—that an early start makes the best of the day, and so I was up and doing by 08.00 hours. The road lay south first, and then circling the open vastness of the Causse to see the old Templar fortress-village of La Couvertoirade, a medieval village, little changed since the Middle Ages. Then down to Le Caylar, and south through St-Pierre-de-la-Fage and across the hills of the Languedoc to Montpeyroux, Aniane, across the Pont de Diable and up and over to the last hill climb, to Montarnaud.

Suddenly, there it was! I looked up through sweaty and sunburnt eyelids at the final flattening of yet another ascent and that had to be it. There, beyond the green flat plain full of vineyards, that blue shimmer was the sea . . .

I had arrived. Now, with the end in sight and even with two days in hand, I had no great desire to hang back. It was evening and, though warm, the worst of the heat was gone. I went up through the gears and raced down the hills, across the roaring traffic which infests the coastal plain and, as the dusk rushed down and all the lights came on, arrived at Palavas-les-Flots and the shores of the Mediterranean.

Tradition may be a fine thing, but sand and salt are not good for bikes. I chained my cycle to a handy railing, trotted down the beach into the sea and, fully clad, sat down among the waves.

La Couvertoirade

After a week in the saddle it seemed the right symbolic gesture!

\* \* \*

A few points. This ride took eight days on the road and I averaged around 120km per day or more. I think that this is too much and would urge the reader to base his or her tours on a daily average of 80km. The motivation in my case, which will not apply to many readers, was that if I pressed on I could catch the earlier boat and join my family that much sooner. Costs averaged £9 per day, much of it on soft drinks, for it was very hot with temperatures averaging 30–35°C for most of the week. That apart I had no problems and only one puncture.

Lessons learned? Only the old, usually ignored ones, but they have stood the test of time and are worth listing once again.
1. Plan your trip and stick to your daily average.
2. Get fit or at least fitter before you leave.
3. Travel light.
4. Start early, and travel on minor roads.
5. Get the cycle ready and take a few spare parts.
6. That done, go, and don't worry.

I have had my say, so goodbye and good luck to you on all your cycletours in France.

# Appendix 1
# REQUEST FOR
# INFORMATION

### English
DearSir/Madam,

I am planning a cycling tour in your region and I would be very grateful for any information or illustrated material you could send me on the available facilities for cycletours and camping in your area.

I already have the IGN maps and the Michelin Guides. Is there any area you would particularly recommend?

I enclose a large stamped addressed envelope, together with an International Reply Coupon for the postage. I look forward to an early reply.

Yours faithfully,<br>
A. N. Other

### French
Monsieur/Madame,

J'ai l'intention d'effectuer une randonnée en vélo dans votre région et je vous serais reconnaissant de toute information et brochures que vous pourriez m'envoyer sur les possibilités de cyclotourisme et de camping dans la région.

Je possède déjà les cartes IGN et les Guides Michelin. Il y a certainement des endroits intéressants?

Je joins une enveloppe à mon adresse et un Coupon-réponse International. Dans l'attente de vous lire, veuillez agréer Madame/Monsieur mes meilleurs sentiments.

A. N. Other

# Appendix 2
# USEFUL WORDS AND PHRASES

## GENERAL

| French | English |
|--------|---------|
| une carte | map |
| tout droit | straight on |
| à droite | turn right |
| à gauche | turn left |
| une tente | tent |
| sac de couchage | sleeping bag |
| un abri | shelter |
| une boulangerie | baker |
| une épicerie | grocer |
| un boucher | a butcher |
| un terrain de camping | campsite |
| un gué | a ford |
| château d'eau | water tower |
| une pharmacie | chemist |
| un coup de soleil | sun stroke |
| une bière | beer |
| bière pression | draft beer |
| un demi | a small beer |
| le temps | the weather |
| beau temps | good weather |
| mauvais temps | bad weather |
| je me suis perdu . . . | I am lost |
| Pouvez-vous m'indiquer le chemin de . . . | Can you show me the way to . . . |
| je suis fatigué | I am tired |

| | |
|---|---|
| je suis épuisé | I am shattered |
| quelle est la distance jusqu'à . . . | How far is it to . . . |
| Une cartouche *or* une recharge | a cartridge (of gas) |
| la neige | snow |
| il'y a . . . | there is . . . |
| activités de plein-air | outdoor activities |
| la boue | mud |
| mouillé | wet |
| une douche | a shower |
| une averse | a shower (of rain) |

## THE FRAME

| | |
|---|---|
| Le cadre | The frame |
| La fourche-avant | The front fork |
| Le guidon | The handlebars |
| Le logement du pédalier | Bottom bracket |
| La selle | Saddle |
| La manivelle | Crank |

## THE WHEEL

| | |
|---|---|
| La roue | The wheel |
| Le pneu | Tyre |
| La chambre à air | Inner tube |
| La jante | Rim |
| Le rayon | Spoke |
| Le moyeu | Hub |
| La valve | Valve |
| L'axe | Axle |
| Le cliquet (les cliquets) | Pawl(s) |
| La noix | Block |
| La denture | Cog |
| Le cone | Cone |
| Le roulement à billes | Ball-bearing |

## ACCESSORIES

| | |
|---|---|
| Les accessoires | Accessories |
| Le timbre; la sonnette | Bell |
| Le garde-boue | Mudguard |

| Le porte-bagages | Pannier Rack |
| La pompe | Pump |
| Le sacoche | Saddle bag |
| Le sac de guidon | Handlebar bag |
| Les paniers | Panniers |
| Les cale-pieds | Toe clips |
| Le truc *or* le machin | The 'thingummybob'; the 'whatsit' |
| Corroies de cale-pieds | Toe straps |
| Le bidon | Water-bottle |

## THE TRANSMISSION

| La transmission | The transmission |
| La chaîne | Chain |
| Le maillon | Chain link |
| Le pédale | Pedal |
| La clavette | Cotter pin |
| Les vitesses méchanism (mécanique) dérailleur | Gears (ratios) |
| Les friens | Brakes |
| L'éclairage | Lights |
| Le phare; le feu avant | Front light |
| Le feu rouge | Rear light |
| Le cable de changement de vitesse | Gear cable |
| Le frein avant/arrière | Brake (front/rear) |
| Le cable | Brake cable |
| Le plomb | Nipple (of cable) |
| Le lévier de frein/poignée | Brake lever |
| La lampe | Lamp |
| La dynamo | Dynamo |
| L'ampoule | Bulb |
| La pile | Battery |
| Le changement de vitesse | Gear change |

## USEFUL ADJECTIVES

| Endoumagé | Damaged |
| Tordu | Bent |
| Cassé | Broken |
| Crevé | Punctured |

| | |
|---|---|
| Eclaté, fendu | Split |
| Endommage, arraché | Stripped |
| Dévissé | Loose |
| Serré | Tight |
| Grippé, bloqué | Stuck |
| Sale, plein de sable | Gritty |
| Avant | Front |
| Arrière | Rear |

## USEFUL VERBS

| | |
|---|---|
| Ajuster, régler | to adjust |
| Nettoyer | to clean |
| Démonter | to dismantle |
| Graisser | to grease |
| Gonfler | to inflate |
| Déserrer | to loosen |
| Baisser | to lower |
| Réparer | to mend |
| Rélever, soulever | to raise |
| Rémonter | to reassemble |
| Visser | to screw |
| Rédresser | to straighten |

## USEFUL SENTENCES

| | |
|---|---|
| Où se trouve un marchand de vélos, s'il vous plaît? | Please direct me to a cycle shop. |
| Réparez-vous les vélos, s'il vous plaît? | Do you repair bicycles? |

# Appendix 3
# COMPANIES OPERATING CYCLING HOLIDAYS IN FRANCE

---

The following companies run cycletouring holidays in France:

**BIKE TOURS**
P.O. Box 75,
Bath BA1 1BX
Avon. Telephone: (0225) 65786.

Susi Madron's Cycling Holidays,
11 Norman Road,
Manchester M14 5LF. Telephone: (061-225) 0739.

Pedals Adventure Cycle Expeditions,
101 Eland Road,
London SW11. Telephone: 01-223 7922.

# BIBLIOGRAPHY

Apart from the titles specifically recommended for each tour, the following are interesting reading.

**ON FRANCE**
**The Conquest of Gaul,** Julius Caesar (Penguin)
**Concise History of France,** Marshall Davidson (Cassell)
**The Devil's Brood,** Alfred Duggan (Faber)
**Traveller's France,** Arthur Eperon (Pan)
**Guide des Logis et Auberges de France** (current edition)
**Guide des Relais Routiers** (current edition)
**A Holiday History of France,** Ronald Hamilton (Chatto & Windus)
**Provençal Sunshine,** Roger Highams (Dent)
**Michelin Green Guides to France** (in French or English)
**Michelin 'Red' Guide** (current edition)
**Fat Man on a Bicycle,** Tom Vernon (Fontana)
**Youth Hosteller's Guide to France** (Y.H.A. Services)
**The Wines of Burgundy,** H. W. Yoxall (Penguin)

**ON CYCLES AND CYCLING**
**Bikepacking,** Robin Adshead (Oxford Illustrated Press)
**Richard's Bicycle Book,** Richard Ballantine (Pan)
**Bicycle Buyer's Guide** (*Bicycle Magazine*)
**Freewheeling,** Raymond Bridge (Stackpole)
**The Young Cyclist's Handbook** (Hamlyn)
**Adventure Cycling,** Tim Hughes (Blandford)
**The Maintenance of Bicycles and Mopeds** (Reader's Digest)

**CYCLING MAGAZINES**
**Bicycle Magazine**
**Bicycle Times**
**Cycletouring**—the magazine of the Cyclists' Touring Club (bi-monthly)
**Cycling**
**Cyclist Monthly**